U0046478

JR Lee

正能量 英文

如果你看過 JR Lee 的影片，你一定會被他那陽光般的笑容給圈粉，從兩歲就和爸媽到美國生活的 JR 有著麻州正港的道地口音，他總是在影片中流利地切換雙語的開關，分享著許多正能量的故事和歌曲，當然有時他也不忘來點英文教學，如果說到英文教學 YouTuber，大家第一印象可能會是阿滴，排名第二的大概就是 JR Lee Radio 了，我的不少學生每週可都殷殷期盼著 JR Lee 的影片，JR 的影片就有如精神食糧般讓他們的心靈得到滋潤。

高中英文教師兼暢銷作家
亡牌教師——戴逸群

如今 JR Lee 化身為暢銷作家和老師，要用最正能量的文章來帶著大家學習英文，從正能量的英文歌曲到感動人心的人物故事，JR 自己書寫每一篇短篇文章，同時搭配文章中生活化的單字用語，透過有趣的方式來學習英文，根本是一個要搶我飯碗的概念。

書中我最喜歡的一個單元就是 JR 的話，不是因為他那賣萌燦笑的 JR 大頭，而是他時而感動人心，時而比較中西文化差異的文字，有時候他也會分享 YouTuber 的小知識，給予想往 YouTuber 道路上前行的莘莘學子一些具體的建議，是書中非常貼心的小安排。

新課綱上路後，素養教學成為教育圈中最火紅的話題，素養的考題又強調真實的情境與學生解決問題的能力，JR 用自身的故事書寫英文文章，用生活化的歌曲來陪伴大家學習英文，真的是非常符合 108 課綱的素養精神，在此要誠摯的推薦這本書給大家，讓我們再一次的被 JR 的正能量感動，讓 JR 也成為你生活中的英文老師！

Hey guys, i

2020 年終於出了我的第一本書，這可是我從二十歲初就設定的人生里程碑之一，如今成就解鎖！把這分喜悅也分享給正在看這本書的你。

我從早期在 ICRT 廣播電臺主持節目時，就在節目裡放了一個叫做「Motto of the Day（**每日座右銘**）」的短單元，希望能幫被上班上學、生活大小事搞得疲憊不堪的聽眾心靈充電。即便離職後，仍然有聽眾寫信跟我說他們有多麼喜歡這個單元。於是我在 2017 年 1 月 1 日正式投入自媒體 YouTube 的行列時，我就期盼能夠繼續帶給大家正能量！

正能量的影片內容在臺灣是一個小眾市場，因此，過程中光是為了讓頻道生存下去，就讓我傷透腦筋。有些系列影片搭配英文，有些搭配時事，有些單純是分享我的平常生活，各個系列各有擁護者。但我很確定的是，無論如何，能夠經營到現在，絕對是因為有你們的支持與愛戴。每當夜深人靜、懷疑人生的時候，我就會想到默默支持我的你們，是的，你們是我不斷做下去的大大動力。

這本書到底是怎樣的一本書呢？一言以蔽之，就是結合「**正能量**」與「**學英文**」的一本書，分為「**正能量英文歌單**」和「**正能量英文文章**」兩個部分。開頭先介紹二十首 JR 我很喜歡的英文流行歌，從邦喬飛、艾薇兒到紅髮艾德、共和世代，每一首歌都是針對某個「症狀」，像孤單、沒人理解、失去親人等特別對症下藥、精挑細選的。我除了會把歌曲的故事細細述說給你聽，還會教你歌詞裡簡單好用的口語片語，裡面的例句對話還是我親自錄音的，很讚吧！（都自己在說！）

第二部分則是我想跟你們分享的二十篇文章故事，前十篇是有關美國時事的文章，後十篇則是我自己親身經歷的正能量故事，全部都是我親自寫的喔！據說出版社的編輯是一邊流下感動的眼淚一邊校稿的（這是她說的，不是我）。文章中的單字和片語，都會搭配有趣的例句，讓你輕鬆記起來。部分文章還附有 QR

's JR!

Code 可以連結到我相對應的 YouTube 影片，當你讀著讀著累了，就可以看看影片休息一下。當然，文章音檔也都是我本人錄製的，個人覺得還頗有誠意的，哈哈。

最後，在享用本書之前，請容許我向你說：「謝謝你的支持！」「有你真好！」並請帶著輕鬆、愉快、沒有負擔的心情，一邊吸收滿滿的正能量，一邊學習英文吧！

PART 1
正能量
英語歌單

❶ 歌曲資訊
左側介紹歌曲資訊與適用症狀，服用時請小心副作用！

❷ YT 影片連結
有些歌曲可以連到我的 YouTube 影片。

❸ 歌曲介紹時間
這裡分享歌曲與歌手背後的故事（跟趣聞！）除了聽歌，你會對這首歌曲有更深一層的認識。

❹ 歌詞中的片語＆例句
這些實用片語會搭配情境對話，讓你知道這些片語到底該怎麼用。

❺ 片語例句音檔
拿起手機掃描 QR Code，就能聽到我親口念例句給你聽。

> 我在對話人物上放入些小巧思，
> 你可以跟著對話慢慢認識這些小人物！

本書特色

USER'S
GUIDE

❶ 正能量座右銘

進入每一篇文章之前，我都會挑選一則跟文章精神符合的 motto，它可以是名人說過的話，也可以是我從過去筆記所記下的話。

> 正能量
> 座右銘
> MOTTO
>
> I don't judge my self-worth as a football player. Football is something I love. It's a fun career deal, but it's not what I want to do with my life because I see football as a game.
>
> 我不會用美式足球員的身分來評價我的自我價值，美式足球是我熱愛的事，是個有趣的職業，但並不是我人生的全部，因為對我來說，美式足球就是個比賽。
>
> — NFL 前紐約噴射機隊四分衛
> Tim Tebow 提姆提伯

> 在頻道敲碗希望我用英文錄影片的，
> 這次算是用文字＋音檔方式，一次滿足你們的願望啦！

The Making of a YouTuber
一個 ▶ YouTuber 的誕生　#01

❷ algorithm
演算法。社群網站的演算法是會影響貼文或影片內容能見度、進而影響廣告曝光、甚至帶來收入的機制

❷ influencer
網紅，原指具有影響力的人，在社群媒體時代就是指「網紅」，也可以說作
social media influencer

❸ vlog
用影片記錄。vlog 是 video blog 的縮寫，就是「影片部落格」，在這裡當動詞用。專門做這件事的人則叫 vlogger，每天做的人稱作 daily vlogger，做這件事為叫做 vlogging

❸ thumbnail
縮圖

Soy Jessi, a young YouTube star, experienced a huge loss of views after she took a break from the *platform. Her mother had *passed away, and so she *took some time off. She came back a few months later, but the views didn't. Maybe that's what happens when you stop feeding the *notorious *algorithm. Or maybe that's just what happens when your *audience *moves on.

It's every social media *influencer's challenge to stay *relevant in the online world. But what is the key factor to having this social media *clout? Is it really all about the algorithm game? Or does quality *content *count?

In his videos, Casey Neistat has repeatedly *brought up his *big break on YouTube. After making videos on the platform for five years, he decided to do daily *vlogging. In a couple of weeks, his channel *exploded. People started noticing his stuff.

So hate it, but *admit it. The algorithm *definitely *plays a role in your online success. That's why YouTubers are *stepping up their game, *cranking new videos out with greater and greater *frequency. In fact, one of the fastest growing Taiwanese YouTubers, Saint (聖結石), *came to fame by uploading daily within the first nine months.

However, you could be doing all the right things—have a crazy uploading schedule, make *eye-catching *thumbnails, write *appealing titles, even *clickbaity ones—but still not get it right. Viewers won't *subscribe if they don't find value in your content,

whether it be entertainment, knowledge, a sense of *company or anything else. It's the algorithm, the thumbnails, the titles that *draw the audience in, but it's the content that makes them stay. No single element stands alone—they all *go hand in hand.

❸ company
陪伴

❸ clickbaity
騙點閱的；蓄意誘導、名詞是 clickbait「騙點閱的圖文標題內容」，由 click（點擊）＋ bait（誘餌）而來

❸ subscribe/unsubscribe
訂閱／取消訂閱。在 YouTube 上對人訂閱影片還這個字。在 Facebook fan page 則 follow/unfollow「追蹤／取消追蹤」，subscriber 則是「訂閱者、訂閱用戶」。

058　JR Lee 正能量英文

059　PART 2 正能量文章　What's Going on Around the World?

---

❷ 主題單字

文章兩側會介紹相關的背景或語言知識。

❸ 正能量文章

就如同我的頻道精神，我希望透過這 20 篇文章，分享時事與自身經歷，帶給你積極正向的能量。

❹ YT 影片連結

點選相關的 YouTube 影片連結，影片文字一起服用，會更有感喔。

❺ JR 的話

我會在這裡分享我對這個議題或現象的想法。

❻ 單字片語

例句是我親自寫的，也是本人親念喔，只要看到書本左頁外側有 QR Code，掃下去就可以聽。有些文章或句子單字會標出底線，那是之前出現過的單字喔。

❼ 延伸學習

每篇文章都有相關主題如「社群媒體」「職場」等，介紹更多實用有趣的英文知識與用語。

Vocabulary & Phrases
單字片語

※ 底線單字與「複習單字」，為之前出現過的字。

1. choir [kwaɪr] (n.)｜唱詩班；合唱團

2. lingering [ˈlɪŋɡərɪŋ] (adj.)｜持續的，揮之不去的

Jack has had lingering nightmares ever since he got into that car accident.
傑克只從出了那場車禍，就不停地被那些揮之不去的惡夢糾纏。

3. on behalf of｜代表；為了⋯⋯的利益

The singer is raising money for charity on behalf of the earthquake victims' families.
那天歌手為了地震受難者家屬的孩童家屬募款。

4. slander [ˈslændər] (v./n.)｜誹謗，詆毀

The newspaper was sued for slander after publishing the fake story about the star.
該報紙因為報導了那則假新聞被該名明星告誹謗。

5. violence [ˈvaɪələns] (n.)｜暴力

People should learn how to settle their arguments without resorting to violence.
人們應該要學習怎麼不用暴力去化解紛爭下的各種爭論。

* resort to｜訴諸，求援於某事；（某種手段）

214　JR Lee 正能量英文

More Expressions
Personality 個性相關單字片語

※ 底線單字與「複習單字」，為之前出現過的字。

帶有正面特質的稱呼

born optimist｜天性樂觀的人	**good egg**｜好人
culture vulture｜熱衷文化藝術的人	**bag egg**｜壞蛋 好東西是形容「好人」，相反地，壞人就是 bad egg。
dark horse｜黑馬	
eager beaver｜拼命工作的人 河狸是一種很勤勞的動物，所以稱的 eager 河狸（beaver）就是形容「工作非常實力、甚至過度的人」。	**go-getter**｜專心致敬的人 形容能定好目標就會達成的人。
early bird｜早起的人 我想早上早起醒，就反過來說 The early bird gets the worm（早起的鳥兒有蟲吃）。	**jack-of-all-trades**｜廣而不精的人 這句諺語人什麼都懂一點但卻無專長，另一個「樣樣通、樣樣鬆」就是英文的 jack-of-all-trades, master of none。
family man/woman｜顧家的人	**man of his word/woman of her word**｜信守承諾的人
smart cookie｜聰明、機靈的人	

帶有負面特質的稱呼

fast-talker｜花言巧語的人 不是形容一人說話很快！而是形容一個人為達目的，很會說服別人說好話來達到他的目的，帶有貶意。	**cheapskate**｜吝嗇鬼，小氣鬼
	goody-goody｜乖寶寶，乖乖牌 喜歡在師長、長官面前當乖寶寶的人。
busybody｜愛多管閒事的人 另一個相似的詞是 meddler。	**gold digger**｜拜金女

205　PART 2 正能量文章　Tell Secret #9

音檔
使用說明

★掃描各頁音檔前，
請先參考本頁說明。

Step-1

掃描書中 QRCode

Step-2

立即註冊

👤 帳號　限3-21碼小寫英文數字

✉ 信箱

🔒 密碼　限8-24碼小寫英文數字

　　　　再次輸入密碼

完成

或

社群帳號註冊

f 使用Facebook註冊

Google　使用Goole註冊

快速註冊或登入 EZCourse

Step-3

請回答以下問題完成訂閱

一、請問本書第65頁，紅色框線中的英
文　　　是什麼？

答案　請注意大小寫

二、請問本書第33頁，紅色框線中的英
文　　　是什麼？

答案　請注意大小寫

送出

回答問題按送出

答案就在書中（需注意空格與大小寫）。

Step-4

完成訂閱

該書右側會顯示「已訂閱」，
表示已成功訂閱，
即可點選播放本書音檔。

Step-5

點選個人檔案

查看「我的訂閱紀錄」
會顯示已訂閱本書，
點選封面可到本書線上聆聽。

Table
of
Contents

目
錄

PART 1
Uplifting Songs
正能量英文歌曲

PART 2
Inspirational Stories
正能量故事

What's Going On Around the World

Table
of
Contents

目
錄

All
About
JR

Uplifting Songs

正能量 英文歌曲

PART 1

It's My Life

Sinatra made 16 movies and toured till he was 80. This is my role model. He (Sambora) said, "You can't write that damn lyric. Nobody cares about Frank Sinatra but you." And I wrote it anyway.

—— **Jon Bon Jovi**

法蘭克辛納屈演出了十六部電影，還一直巡演到八十歲為止，他是我的模範，而他（吉他手山伯拉）說，「你不能寫下那該死的歌詞，除了你沒人在乎法蘭克辛納屈」，結果我還是寫了。

—— 瓊邦喬飛

製造廠商：Bon Jovi 邦喬飛
藥品屬性：搖滾
出廠年分：2000 年
副作用：亢奮．失眠．失控猛點頭
適用症狀：遭受挫折，覺得自己是魯蛇時

邦喬飛（Bon Jovi）團員自 1995 年休息近五年之後，在 1999 年重新合體，在隔年出了他們睽違已久的新專輯《Crush》，首支單曲〈It's My Life〉成了他們在國際樂壇上表現最為亮眼的單曲，並且成功吸引新世代的年輕樂迷，讓邦喬飛成為歷久不衰的搖滾樂團。

〈It's My Life〉裡有許多他們 1986 年冠軍單曲〈Livin' On A Prayer〉的影子。首先，歌詞再次提到 Tommy 和 Gina 這兩個人。主唱瓊邦喬飛（Jon Bon Jovi）表示，當初寫〈Livin' On A Prayer〉，是受到共同創作人 Desmond Child 自身故事的啟發。70 年代晚期，他曾在紐約開計程車維生，當時的女朋友 Maria 則是在餐廳端盤子，這兩人化身為歌詞裡的 Tommy 和 Gina 這對為了生活而掙扎奮鬥的情侶。相隔 14 年，又再次出現在邦喬飛的歌詞中。此外，神級吉他手山伯拉（Richie Sambora，2013 年已離團）在這首歌裡也重現當年的 Talkbox 效果器音效，給人一種新穎又經典再現的感覺。

副歌裡有一句歌詞：Like Frankie said, "I did it my way."（就像法蘭克說的，「我用我自己的方式做到了。」）則是主唱 Jon Bon Jovi 向同為紐澤西人的 Frank Sinatra（法蘭克辛納屈）翻唱的經典老歌〈My Way〉致敬。

〈It's My Life〉之所以成功，是因為歌詞引起廣大聽眾共鳴，從青少年到成年人，都感受到那種「這是我的人生，我要掌握自己的人生方向盤」的感覺。加上熱血的搖滾節奏，使這首歌成為邦喬飛最經典的搖滾國歌。

DJ JR 歌曲介紹時間

001

▶ 歌詞中值得學習的單字片語 ◀

因為歌詞版權的緣故，本部分無法寫上完整的歌詞內容喔，喜歡歌曲的話，可以自己上網去查喔！

---

1. stand one's ground ｜堅守立場，拒不讓步

---

2. back down ｜認錯；認輸；退卻

| Jack: | Why didn't you stand your ground at the meeting? | 傑克：你為什麼沒有在會議中堅持立場？ |
| Tommy: | The only reason I backed down is because you didn't back me up! | 湯米：我之所以讓步，還不都是因為你沒有支持我！ |

* back sb. up ｜支持某人

Jack:	You should have stood your ground before Gina.	傑克：你在吉娜面前應該要堅守立場的。
Tommy:	I had to back down. You don't understand.	湯米：我非得讓步不可，你不懂啦。
Jack:	Why? What don't I understand?	傑克：為什麼？我到底不懂什麼？
Tommy:	Gina.	湯米：吉娜。

---

3. call sb. out ｜公開批評某人；要求某人解釋自己行為；挑戰某人

Bob:	Did you see the way the manager was talking to Mary? He was so rude.	鮑伯：你有看到經理是怎麼跟瑪麗講話的嗎？超沒禮貌。
Tommy:	Yeah. Somebody needs to call him out on his bad behavior.	湯米：是啊。應該要有人叫他為自己的行為解釋一下。
Bob:	Not me. I need this job!	鮑伯：可別叫我。我還需要這份工作。

#02 Stacie Orrico

(There's Gotta Be) More to Life

適用症狀：空虛，找不到人生意義時

副作用：對著月亮發呆，坐在馬桶上沉思人生

出廠年分：2003 年

藥品屬性：流行、R&B

製造廠商：Stacie Orrico 甜檸檬史黛西

I'm not driven by the kudos and awards and accolades...
I definitely do it for the people I'm trying to speak to.

—— Stacie Orrico

驅使我前進的不是名聲、獎項或他人的讚美……我是為了我想影響的人們而創作。

—— 甜檸檬史黛西

DJ JR
歌曲
介紹時間

在 2000 年代那個小甜甜布蘭妮（Britney Spears）、克莉絲汀（Christina Aguilera）、珍妮佛羅培茲（Jennifer Lopez）等眾多強力女星捉對廝殺的時期，有個 17 歲的小女生默默地浮出了檯面。甜檸檬史黛西（Stacie Orrico）忽然間成了一個大家熱烈討論的名字，2003 年她發了第二張同名專輯，全球賣了三百五十萬張，單曲〈Stuck〉、〈(There's Gotta Be) More to Life〉在 MTV 頻道上瘋狂播放，當年我最喜歡的就是後者，也就是要跟你們介紹的歌。

史黛西在教會詩班長大，在六歲時寫下第一首歌。受到家庭和信仰的影響，她曾經在烏克蘭傳了一年的福音，而且始終跟家人保持密切關係。早期史黛西也曾跟當年火紅的天命真女（Destiny's Child）共同巡演，從中她體會到，無論膚色、宗教、文化背景再怎麼不同，青少年都有相似的煩惱。可惜的是，史黛西在發行第三張專輯之後就淡出樂壇。期間她返回校園讀書進修，也飛到非洲當志工。即便 2013 年，她在 YouTube 頻道上宣布即將重返錄音室，但至今仍沒有進一步消息。

我之所以很喜歡〈(There's Gotta Be) More to Life〉這首歌，除了旋律和史黛西厚實高亢的聲音之外，更是因為富有內涵的歌詞：There's gotta be more to life than chasing down every temporary high to satisfy me.（比起只是為了滿足自己而不斷追逐著生命中一次又一次的短暫高潮，人生中應該有更有意義的事。）年輕的時候聽到這首歌，我總不禁看著夜空中的月亮，心想，「我的人生不該只是如此而已」。

▶ 歌詞中值得學習的單字片語 ◀

1. let sth. go │ 放手；釋懷，不再擔憂

....

2. trip out │（口語）因害怕或擔心而失控，類似 freak out。

....

Tommy:	You really need to let go of that bad breakup.
Bob:	It's so hard to let go. Every time I think about it, I start tripping out.

Jack:	Bob's tripping out about someone making fun of his new haircut.
Tommy:	Man, he really needs to let it go.

湯米：你真的該釋懷分手的事了。
鮑伯：好難放手，每當我想起就會開始發慌。

傑克：鮑伯因為有人嘲笑他的新髮型而抓狂。
湯米：老兄，他真的要學會放下。

* make fun of sb. │ 取笑某人，開某人玩笑

#03 Kelly Clarkson

Breakaway

I had no idea what the show was until the third audition. My goal was just to be a backup singer—I never intended to be in front. But then my apartment in L.A. burned down and I had to move home, I had no money and I had to sleep in my car for three days. I just auditioned for this thing that said they'd pay you, and it happened to be *American Idol*.

— Kelly Clarkson

直到第三次試鏡，我才知道這是什麼節目。我的目標單純只是想成為和聲歌手，我從沒想過要站在前面。但是接著我在洛杉磯的公寓發生火災，我不得不搬回家，我身無分文，只得在車上睡了三天。我去參加這個他們說有錢可以拿的試鏡，沒想到就是《美國偶像》。

— 凱莉克萊森

適用症狀：感到迷惘，前途茫茫；失去勇氣時

副作用：彈空氣吉他；破音（請在無人空間服用）

出廠年分：2004 年

藥品屬性：流行

製造廠商：Kelly Clarkson 凱莉克萊森

這首歌的歌詞其實是艾薇兒（Avril Lavigne）寫的，不過當時發現這首歌並不適合收錄在她準備發行的第二張專輯，於是就給了凱莉克萊森（Kelly Clarkson）。其實不難想像艾薇兒唱這首輕搖滾流行歌的樣子，完全沒有違和感，而且網路上也找得到她演唱的版本喔！

歌詞唱述著脫離舊有的自己與生活，不計代價尋求改變、冒險，蛻變成一個嶄新的自己：I'll spread my wings and I'll learn how to fly; I'll do what it takes till I touch the sky.（我會展開雙翼，學會飛翔，我會不計一切代價，直到我飛上雲端。）雖然這是艾薇兒自己的心路歷程，但是 Kelly 對這首歌也有著強烈的共鳴。她為了追尋音樂夢而放棄大學獎學金，從家鄉德州跑到光芒四射的洛杉磯，幾經挫折，被無數唱片公司拒絕後又回到家鄉打零工，直到 2002 年選秀節目第一屆《美國偶像》到德州達拉斯選秀，Kelly 一路過關斬將，最終拿下冠軍，從此在樂壇展露頭角。

〈Breakaway〉之所以給 Kelly，也是為了錄製安海瑟威（Anne Hathaway）主演的《麻雀變公主 2》電影原聲帶。沒想到獲得極大迴響，因而收錄在 Kelly 的第二張專輯，專輯名稱也同樣以〈Breakaway〉命名。這是 Kelly 第三首進入告示牌百大單曲榜前十名的單曲，如果你也正在經歷轉變，需要脫胎換骨，這首勵志歌正適合你。

DJ JR
歌曲
介紹時間

▶ 歌詞中值得學習的單字片語 ◀

1. reach out (to sb.) | （向某人）主動伸出援手

也有「接觸某人或某群體」、「跟某人打成一片」的意思。

2. speak up/out | 公開發表意見，坦率說出

通常是針對有強烈情感共鳴的話題。

3. take a chance / take chances | 冒險

Jenny: We need to reach out to the younger generation if we want this new product to succeed.

Jack: Thank you for speaking up, Jenny. Does everybody agree we should take a chance on this?

珍妮：如果新產品要成功，我們應該要將觸角伸向年輕族群。

傑克：感謝珍妮發表意見，大家都同意我們該試試看嗎？

#04 Simple Plan

Perfect

When we played 'Perfect,' a lot of them were crying. They weren't crying hysterically like with the Beatles where it's like, "I love you!" It was more the emotion from the lyrics and how they could relate to it.

—— **Pierre Bouvier**

當我們演唱〈Perfect〉時，許多人哭了。他們不是像看見披頭四時歇斯底里地哭喊著「我愛你！」而是出自於對歌詞所產生的情緒與共鳴而哭。

—— 主唱皮耶

適用症狀：得不到父母認同，失去信心時
副作用：多愁善感；鄰居檢舉噪音妨害安寧
出廠年分：2002 年
藥品屬性：龐克搖滾
製造廠商：Simple Plan 簡單樂團

回想我的學生時期，半夜聽著簡單樂團（Simple Plan）的龐克搖滾樂，邊點頭邊放聲嘶吼，雖然現在已經回不去，但每當聽到他們的音樂，就會有種懷念的感覺。2000 年代是龐克搖滾樂大放異采的時期，出現許多知名樂團如 Good Charlotte、Sum 41、blink-182，而其中 Simple Plan 絕對是家喻戶曉的團名。特別是他們這首〈Perfect〉，打中了當時無數青少年的心。

這首歌的靈感來自於鼓手查克（Chuck Comeau）跟他父母之間的緊張關係。當時父母親希望他有穩定職業，因此不支持他追求音樂。Cause we lost it all, nothing lasts forever. I'm sorry I can't be perfect.（因為我們失去了一切，沒有一件事物會永遠存在，我很抱歉我並不完美。）唱出了內心深處對父母的心聲，相信當年的歌迷仍對這句歌詞耳熟能詳。這首歌的不插電版本還收錄在琳賽蘿涵（Lindsay Lohan）主演的《高校天后》（*Confessions of a Teenage Drama Queen*）電影原聲帶中。

主唱皮耶（Pierre Bouvier）說，他第一次見識到這首歌的感染力是在早期的演唱會上，當時前排站著的都是年輕人，特別是女生，她們邊唱邊落下眼淚。

轉眼間已經來到 2020 年，當年的龐克小伙子，現在也成為人父。Pierre 接受採訪時說：「這首歌讓我想起自己小時候，讓我用不同角度面對自己的孩子。我期許自己像〈Perfect〉這首歌，當我跟子女關係緊張時，能夠寬容地對待他們，讓我能夠想起過去那段歲月的我自己，為了要造就自己、學習成為一個合宜的人，那時候會有許多困或以及該要學習的

**DJ JR
歌曲
介紹時間**

▶ 歌詞中值得學習的單字片語 ◀

1. make sb. proud │ 讓某人引以為傲

2. be good enough (for sb./sth.) │（對某人某事來說）已足夠滿意

I try to make my parents proud (of me), but nothing I do seems to be good enough for them.
我想讓我爸媽（對我）感到驕傲，但不論我做什麼，他們好像都覺得不夠。

3. turn one's back (on sb./sth.) │ 轉身背對；拒絕幫助、支持或參與某人某事

Jenny: So what did Kathy say when you asked her out?

Bob: Nothing. She just turned her back and walked away.

Jenny: Wow. I heard Kathy was an ice queen, but that's really cold.

Bob: Tell me about it.

珍妮：所以你約凱西出去時她說了什麼？

鮑伯：什麼都沒說。她只是轉頭就走。

珍妮：哇，我是有聽說凱西是冰山，不過這樣做真的很冷酷。

鮑伯：這還用說。

* **ice queen** │ 冰山美人

* **tell me about it** │（口語）這還用說，表示知道狀況有多糟。

#05 Natasha Bedingfield
Unwritten

適用症狀：年少無知，感到徬徨時
副作用：自律神經失調；手舞足蹈
出廠年分：2004 年
藥品屬性：流行
製造廠商：Natasha Bedingfield 娜塔莎貝汀菲兒

I really started to have dreams for myself when I was 17, but I was always afraid people were going to laugh at me. I finally just said, "All right. I'm going to write songs, even if they're bad. I'm just going to keep writing until I get good."

—— **Natasha Bedingfield**

我從十七歲開始有自己的夢想，但我始終害怕別人嘲笑我，終於有一天我對自己說：「好吧，我要寫歌了，就算寫得很糟，我就一直寫到我變厲害為止。」

—— 娜塔莎貝汀菲兒

英國流行歌手娜塔莎貝汀菲兒（Natasha Bedingfield）在 2004 年以專輯〈Unwritten〉初試啼聲，立即獲得廣大迴響，專輯同名單曲獲得葛萊美獎最佳流行女歌手提名、全英音樂獎等多項提名，還成為 2006 年度美國廣播電臺最常播放歌曲，另一首〈These Words〉則成了她第一支英國單曲排行榜冠軍；另一個幫助〈Unwritten〉奠定流行基礎的是 MTV 頻道的實境電視節目《The Hills》，當年節目片頭曲就選用了這首歌，並且在片尾時還置入了歌曲 MV 片段。

事實上，〈Unwritten〉是 Natasha 送給當時過十四歲生日的弟弟的生日禮物，她身上沒什麼錢，於是索性寫了這首關於「把生命活到最滿」的歌，Feel the rain on your skin. No one else can feel it for you, only you can let it in... Today is where your book begins. The rest is still unwritten.（感受落在你肌膚上的雨，沒有人能代替你感受，唯有你自己能……今天是你書本的開端，其餘的等待你去寫滿。）Natasha 說：「他（弟弟）的生活使我想起，人們是如何認為我們必須要把一切都想清楚，我們必須要想好自己要上哪間大學、要主修什麼課。然而，我們甚至連人生都還搞不大懂是怎麼一回事。」

DJ JR 歌曲介紹時間

▶ 歌詞中值得學習的單字片語 ◀

1. read one's mind｜看出某人的心思

....

2. reach for sth.｜為了得到或觸碰到某事物而伸出手

....

(Tommy reaches out his hand to Gina.)

Tommy: Can you read my mind? What am I reaching for?

Gina: You're reaching for my love. Right, honey?

Tommy: Actually, I was just reaching for the phone. Could you pass it to me?

（湯米向吉娜伸出手。）

湯米： 妳能讀出我的內心嗎？我伸手要什麼？

吉娜： 你伸手想要得到我的愛，對吧，親愛的？

湯米： 其實，我是想要拿電話啦，妳可以遞給我嗎？

....

3. let sb./sth. in｜接納某人某事

衍伸為「讓某人某事物進入自己的內心，接納某人某事物」的意思。

Tommy: Would you please let me in?

Gina: In where? We're in the same office, silly.

Tommy: Inside your heart.

湯米： 拜託妳，可以讓我進去嗎？

吉娜： 進去哪？笨蛋，我們在同一間辦公室耶。

湯米： 進去妳心裡。

#06 John Mayer
No Such Thing

Well I never lived the dreams of the prom kings and the drama queens. I'd like to think the best of me is still hiding up my sleeve.

—— 〈**No Such Thing**〉John Mayer

我不曾有過像舞會的舞王、舞后般夢幻的生活。我自認我一手好牌還藏在袖口裡。

—— 〈No Such Thing〉約翰梅爾

適用症狀：懷才不遇
沒有人欣賞自己，待價而沽時
副作用：自我感覺良好；自戀症候群
出廠年分：2002 年
藥品屬性：流行搖滾
製造廠商：John Mayer 約翰梅爾

經常在採訪時語出驚人、令人尷尬兼錯愕不已的 John Mayer，其實剛出道時的音樂充滿著青春單純、天真的氛圍。〈No Such Thing〉是他首張專輯的主打單曲，也是幫助他在歌壇打響名號的歌。當時這首歌還登上美國告示牌百大單曲第十三名，五年後他才以〈Say〉打破了自己的榜單紀錄。

不像大部分的同學在高中畢業後就上大學，John 選擇打工存錢，買了把吉他。雖然在父母的極力勸說之下，終究還是勉強讀了伯克立音樂學院（Berklee College of Music）。不過讀了兩個學期之後，他就跟好朋友 Clay Cook 休學，跑去追逐音樂夢想了。這首〈No Such Thing〉就是反映出他高中時期青春叛逆、勇於追夢的心境。

當大家叫他要循規蹈矩、跟著前人的路走，John 則大聲唱說：「我發現根本沒有所謂『現實世界』這件事，這只不過是一個你必須要超越的謊言。」（I just found out there's no such thing as the real world. Just a lie you've got to rise above.）

JR 我在學生時期超喜歡這首歌，有種抒發自己懷才不遇（雖然其實沒什麼才）的感覺，等待有一天能抓住機會、一鳴驚人！如果你也在等待證明自己的那一天來到，那這首歌正適合你！

DJ JR 歌曲介紹時間

▶ 歌詞中值得學習的單字片語 ◀

1. have sth. up one's sleeve｜留一手；深藏不露

sleeve 是「袖子」，在袖子裡面藏著什麼東西，表示有一個祕密的計劃或點子還藏而未用。
歌詞裡用 hide up one's sleeve，刻意強調他「藏」而未用。

Gina:	The rent is due and we don't get paid till next week! What are we gonna do?
Tommy:	No worries, babe. I've got a little money up my sleeve.
Gina:	Wait... you've been hiding money from me?

吉娜：該繳房租了，但是我們下禮拜才領薪水，怎麼辦？

湯米：別擔心，寶貝，我有點私房錢。

吉娜：等等……你竟然偷偷藏錢？

2. stay inside the lines｜謹守規矩或分寸

保持在線（line）內，原意是來自於叫小朋友著色時，不要超出著色本裡頭的線條
（color inside the lines），衍伸為「不要違反規則或常規」的意思。

Son:	Mom, I hate school! All the teachers do is force us to color inside the lines!
Mom:	Watch your attitude, young man. You're in school to learn discipline.

兒子：媽，我超討厭學校！學校老師成天到晚只會叫我們要安分守己！

媽媽：注意你的態度，年輕人，你去上學就是要學紀律。

3. at the top of one's lungs/voice｜用最大的聲音

把肺（lungs）用到最高極限，也就是「以最大的聲音」的意思。

(at a restaurant)	
Gina:	Why are those guys sitting over there singing at the top of their lungs like this is karaoke night?
Jenny:	Wait, is that Bob and Tommy?

（在餐廳）

吉娜：坐在那裡的傢伙們幹嘛這麼大聲唱歌，一副把這裡當作卡拉 OK 之夜啊？

珍妮：等一下，那是鮑伯和湯米嗎？

#07 Gym Class Heroes ft. Ryan Tedder
The Fighter

Definitely a very motivational, inspirational kind of song.

—— Travie McCoy

這絕對是一首非常勵志、鼓舞人心的歌。

—— 主唱崔維

適用症狀：遭受挫折，不被看好時
副作用：熱血澎派性高血壓；假音唱不上去；高音性臉部抽筋
出廠年分：2011 年
藥品屬性：流行，饒舌
製造廠商：Gym Class Heroes ft. Ryan Tedder
體育課英雄樂團 ft. 萊恩泰德

你也許沒聽過體育課英雄樂團（Gym Class Heroes）（真的嗎？）但你在逛街時八成有聽過〈Cupid's Chokehold〉、〈Ass Back Home〉，或是跟魔力紅（Maroon 5）主唱亞當（Adam Levine）合作的〈Stereo Hearts〉這些膾炙人口的歌。而與後者收錄於同一張專輯的〈The Fighter〉，絕對是一首適合在遭受挫折、處於低潮、需要力量時所聆聽的歌。主唱崔維（Travie McCoy）接受告示牌雜誌專訪時說道：「這首歌就像是踹我屁股似地在提醒我，這一路走來，我和樂團真的非常非常努力才達到今天的成就，也提醒著我，不要鬆懈。希望這首歌能鼓舞年輕人，要對他們所愛之事堅持不懈，並告訴他們努力會有回報。不是要故意講得很落俗套啦，但就是……（你知道的）」。

共和世代（OneRepublic）主唱萊恩（Ryan Tedder）跨刀幫忙寫作、製作並演唱，為整首歌曲加分一百倍！畢竟 Ryan 幫人寫歌總有點石成金的魔力，碧昂絲（Beyoncé）的〈Halo〉、里歐娜露維絲（Leona Lewis）的〈Bleeding Love〉，跟紅髮艾德（Ed Sheeran）合寫的〈Happier〉等，這些不過只是冰山一角。

歌曲 MV 是以半紀錄片的方式，記錄美國奧運體操選手 John Orozco 奮戰的歷程，中間不時穿插 Travie McCoy 和 Ryan Tedder 的演唱畫面，邊聽歌邊看 MV，絕對會讓你熱血沸騰！

DJ JR
歌曲
介紹時間

▶ 歌詞中值得學習的單字片語 ◀

1. be honest with sb. | 跟某人誠實以對

2. be better off | 在……情況下更好

3. give sb. hell | 讓某人受苦；大罵某人

Bob:	I came in 10 minutes late, and Jack gave me hell for it!
Tommy:	Don't feel bad. He does that to everybody. He can't stand tardiness.
Bob:	That makes me feel a little better. I guess I'd better get new batteries for my alarm clock.

鮑伯：我遲到十分鐘，傑克就把我罵得臭頭！
湯米：別難過了，他對誰都這樣。他無法容忍別人遲到。
鮑伯：這樣我心情有好一點。我得幫我的鬧鐘換電池了。

* **tardiness** [`tɑrdɪnɪs] (n.) | 拖拖拉拉，遲到，形容詞是 tardy。

4. turn (people's) heads | 吸引目光

該片語意思是「人們因為驚訝、感到興趣、被吸引而轉過頭來看；引起很大的注意」。
head-turning 則是其形容詞，「吸引人的」意思。

Bob's new sports car is really turning heads.
鮑伯的新跑車真的很吸睛。

Jenny wore a head-turning red silk dress to the party.
珍妮穿了一套吸睛的紅色絲綢洋裝來參加派對。

#08 The Script

Superheroes

There's people being bullied and sold to the sex slave trade, yet they remain optimistic and positive. They're unsung heroes.

—— Danny O'Donoghue

他們之中有人遭到霸凌、被賣去從事性交易，然而他們仍保持樂觀正向，他們是未被歌頌的英雄。

—— 主唱丹尼

適用症狀：妄自菲薄，自覺平庸

副作用：喉嚨撕裂傷；手握麥克風幻想症

出廠年分：2014 年

藥品屬性：流行搖滾

製造廠商：The Script 手創樂團

JR YouTube
影片 #1

某次演唱會結束後，The Script 手創樂團主唱丹尼（Danny O'Donoghue）在後臺亢奮地跟團員們叫囂著一些拳王阿里式的垃圾話，Danny 說：「就只是在胡鬧，所以我們試著把那感覺記錄下來，寫成歌詞。」

〈Superheroes〉是一首激勵人心的流行搖滾歌曲，歌詞描述著在這世上掙扎奮鬥、晝夜不停息地為了生活而打拼的人們。MV 在南非約翰尼斯堡拍攝，他們在一個人口只有 20 萬、相當貧困的城鎮架起舞臺，帶起一股嘉年華會的氣氛，主唱 Danny 說：「我們度過了不可思議的一段時光，我們花了幾天時間在那裡，跟城裡的人們相處了很久，因為他們是我們的超級英雄，是經歷極為艱困的時刻卻仍然不被打倒的人。基本上，這首歌就是在傳達這個訊息。」在採訪中他也提到，「他們之中有些人遭到霸凌、被販賣去從事性交易，然而他們仍保持樂觀正向，他們是未被歌頌的英雄。」

JR 我也曾在 2018 年 The Script 臺灣巡迴演唱時，有幸在臺灣大學體育館的後臺採訪了他們，三位團員 Danny、Mark、Glen 都是關懷社會議題、充滿正能量的人，而且很搞笑，哈哈哈！可以在我的頻道 JR Lee Radio 上看到我對 The Script 的專訪喔！

DJ JR
歌曲
介紹時間

▶ 歌詞中值得學習的單字片語 ◀

1. fight for sth. │ 為了某事而戰；爭取某事

2. make sth. right │ 把某事做對；彌補某事

Bob: I know I blew it. How can I make it right?

Tommy: If you really want something, you have to go fight for it!

鮑伯：我知道我搞砸了，我該怎麼挽回？

湯米：如果你真的很想要，就要去爭取！

* **blow it** │（口語）搞砸了

3. turn sth. into sth. │ 把某事轉變成某事

Tommy: If only I could turn my belly into six-pack abs like Chris Hemsworth has.

Gina: If only I could turn you into Chris!

湯米：要是我可以把肚子變成像克里斯漢斯沃（雷神索爾）的六塊肌有多好。

吉娜：要是我可以把你變成克里斯有多好！

* **six-pack abs** │ 六塊肌

#09 Alicia Keys
Underdog

Some people may think of the word "underdog" as a negative word. But I see it as a powerful word representing people who may be underestimated and yet still rise to the challenge and exceed expectations.

—— **Alicia Keys**

有些人會覺得「劣勢者」是個負面用詞，但我看來，它是一個帶有力量的字，代表那些被低估卻仍舊面對挑戰，並努力超越期待的人。

—— 艾莉西亞凱斯

適用症狀：被低估；身處逆境
副作用：中毒式身體左右搖擺
出廠年分：2020 年
藥品屬性：流行；R&B
製造廠商：Alicia Keys 艾莉西亞凱斯

R&B 天后艾莉西亞凱斯（Alicia Keys）2001 年首張專輯，甫一推出就獲得空前成功，全球狂賣超過 1800 萬張，拿下五項葛萊美獎，單曲〈No One〉至今仍是經典，成為她首支告示牌百大單曲排行榜冠軍。

兩年後推出第二張專輯，再次橫掃全球，又為她增添了四座葛萊美獎，2004 年跟亞瑟小子（Usher）合唱的〈My Boo〉是當時大街小巷都絕對聽得到的熱門歌曲，也成為了她第二支百大單曲冠軍，能夠看到 Alicia Keys 在 2020 年持續發新專輯，實屬一件令人興奮的事！

歌曲〈Underdog〉的靈感來自於 Alicia 自幼的生長環境，她在單親家庭長大，從小住在紐約市曼哈頓的貧民區，但是先天不良的環境並沒有擊倒她。透過這首歌，她想傳達給那些被輕忽、低估的人一個訊息：「別讓逆境阻礙了你追求目標的熱情。」This goes out to the underdog. Keep on keeping at what you love. You'll find that someday soon enough you will rise up.（這首歌送給那些劣勢者，繼續堅持你所愛的，你會發現，很快地你將會掘起。）。順帶一提，這首歌是 Alicia 跟紅髮艾德一起寫的。

DJ JR 歌曲介紹時間

▶ 歌詞中值得學習的單字片語 ◀

※ 底線單字為「複習單字」，為之前出現過的字。

1. make it｜（口語）（在困難的狀況中）成功

Jack:　　We <u>took our chances</u> and it worked.

Tommy:　I can't believe we made it!

傑克：我們賭了一把，結果成功了。

湯米：我不敢相信我們做到了！

2. break the mold (of sth.)｜打破窠臼，打破常規

mold 是「模子，鑄模」，所以 break the mold（打破模子）就是說「突破既定框架」之意。

Seinfeld broke the mold of TV comedy.

《歡樂單身派對》打破了當時電視喜劇的窠臼。

3. on the run｜逃亡，躲避（警察或權力單位）

The activist has been on the run ever since <u>speaking out</u> against government corruption.

自從該社運人士發聲指責政府貪污，就一直逃亡到現在。

* **activist** [ˈæktəvɪst]｜社會運動人士

#10 Avril Lavigne

Head Above Water

適用症狀：失去力量，徹底絕望時
副作用：熱淚盈眶；眼屎變多；怕水
出廠年分：2018 年
藥品屬性：流行搖滾
製造廠商：Avril Lavigne 艾薇兒

One night I thought I was dying, and I had accepted that I was going to die. Under my breath, I prayed, "God, please help to keep my head above the water."

—— **Avril Lavigne**

有一晚我真的感覺快要死了，而我坦然接受了我的命運，以微微的氣音，我禱告著：「神啊，拜託祢讓我活下去。」

—— 艾薇兒

艾薇兒自從 2013 年發行了同名專輯後便淡出歌壇，在 2015 年短暫以一首獻給殘障奧運的單曲〈Fly〉浮出水面，但隨即又消失在茫茫歌海之中。自此謠言四起，甚至有人說艾薇兒早就死了，而現在四處活動的是她的替身，諸如此類。然而，事實是艾薇兒在 2014 那年，也是她三十歲生日時，被診斷罹患萊姆病，而且病情迅速惡化。她離開歌壇是為了養病，而那段時間，她靠著寫音樂來度過毫無希望的時光。

艾薇兒寫給粉絲的信上寫著，〈Head Above Water〉是有關她與萊姆病的奮戰，而這也是她臥病在床期間所寫下的第一首歌，在一段採訪中她也透露了當時的心境：「有一晚我真的感覺快要死了，而我也坦然接受了我的命運……我母親讓我躺在床上並且抱著我，我感覺像是溺水了一樣，以微微的氣音，我禱告：『神啊，拜託祢讓我活下去。』這首歌就是在那刻誕生的。」

寫完歌詞之後，艾薇兒得到 We The Kings 樂團主唱特拉維斯（Travis Clark）的幫助，而完成了整首歌，在日本銷售的專輯，有一首 bonus track 就是 Travis 幫艾薇兒合音的版本。

DJ JR 歌曲介紹時間

▶ 歌詞中值得學習的單字片語 ◀

1. keep it together ｜保持鎮定

fall apart 是「瓦解、倒塌或崩潰」的意思，那麼不讓它瓦解、崩塌就是 keep it together，
意思就是「保持鎮定、鎮靜」。
類似的用法則有 pull oneself together 或 hold oneself together。

Tommy: Hey, don't let Jack get to you. You gotta keep it together, man!	**湯米：** 嘿，不要被傑克嚇到，你得保持鎮定啊，老兄！
Bob: I know, I know. It's just that every time he talks down to me like that, I start to lose it.	**鮑伯：** 我知道，我知道，只是每當他用居高臨下的口氣跟我說話，我就會抓狂。

* **get to sb.** ｜對某人產生（負面）影響；使某人難受或不舒服

* **talk down to sb.** ｜以居高臨下的口氣對某人說話

* **lose it** ｜（口語）失去理智；發脾氣

2. keep one's head above water ｜勉強支撐下去

讓頭維持在水面之上，就是不讓自己溺水，所以這片語的意思就是「勉強支撐下去」，
特別常用來形容財務方面，歌詞裡則是形容人為了生命、生活而掙扎著。

Mom: We're barely making ends meet. What should we do?	**媽媽：** 我們生活支出幾乎是勉強打平。我們該怎麼辦？
Dad: I don't know. I'm working day and night, and we're barely keeping our heads above water.	**爸爸：** 我不知道，我已經日以繼夜工作，還是只能勉強維持生計。

* **make ends meet** ｜使收支平衡

#11 OneRepublic
Connection

適用症狀：孤單，空虛；過度依賴社群媒體

副作用：說話不自覺用假音

出廠年分：2018 年

藥品屬性：流行

製造廠商：OneRepublic 共和世代

The whole album is steering towards connection. It's about wanting real human connection in a meaningful way because that's really all that matters at the end of the day.

— Ryan Tedder

整張專輯是朝「人與人之間的聯繫」這個方向來寫的，是關乎想得到人與人之間真正有意義的連結，因為到頭來，最重要的莫過於此。

— 主唱萊恩

JR YouTube
影片 #2

共和世代（OneRepublic）出道至今，創作了不少膾炙人口的流行歌，其中許多是關於人生信念、夢想與現實。主唱萊恩泰德（Ryan Tedder）接受告示牌雜誌採訪時曾說：「我認為這是我們身為樂團的責任，也是讓我們得以與眾不同之處。二十年前我還是 U2 的小粉絲時，我從他們身上學到了這一點。」後來當他們有機會跟過往的偶像 U2 樂團巡演時，Ryan 也跟 U2 主唱波諾（Bono）聊到了這一點，並且相談甚歡。Ryan 說：「我感受到一股責任，要寫下並且唱出關乎『人』的歌。如果所有人都唱著男歡女愛、愛情、慾望、金錢，那也要有人唱出關於人生、信念、希望這一類的事吧。」

〈Connection〉的歌詞是 Ryan 自身感觸的投射，If there's so many people here, then why am I so lonely?（如果這裡有這麼多人，那為什麼我還感到無比孤單？）談論起這首歌，他提到：「對我來說，這真的就是我們的現況，以我身為一個「人」的經驗，我想要傳達的就是這個。整張專輯都是朝向『連結』這個方向所寫，是關乎想得到人跟人之間真正有意義的連結，因為到頭來，最重要的莫過於此。」

DJ JR
歌曲
介紹時間

▶ 歌詞中值得學習的單字片語 ◀

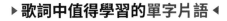

※ 底線單字為「複習單字」，為之前出現過的字。

1. let's face it │ 面對現實吧

face sth. 是「面對某事」的意思，let's face it 是口語表達，
意思是「讓我們面對現實吧！我們實話實說吧！」

Mom:	Let's face it. We both know that if you don't get a raise, by next year we won't have a roof over our heads.
Dad:	I fought for it so many times, but my boss just won't budge.

媽媽：	面對現實吧，你我都知道，如果你再沒加薪，明年我們連住的地方都沒了。
爸爸：	我爭取了好幾次，但老闆就是不為所動。

* **budge** [bʌdʒ] (v.) │ 改變心意，常以否定表達「不為所動」。budge 可作為及物（vt.）與不及物動詞（vi.），
  例句中的用法為不及物用法。

2. paint a... picture (of sth.) │（將某事）描述得很……

paint a rosy picture 的 rosy 指「樂觀、美好的」，所以整句就是「畫大餅」的意思。

Bob:	Jack always paints a rosy picture of the company's future in the meetings.
Tommy:	To be honest with you, I think he's just brown-nosing the boss.

鮑伯：	傑克在會議上總是把公司前景講得有多美好。
湯米：	老實跟你說，我覺得他是在拍老闆馬屁。

* **brown-nose** [braʊn noz] (v.) │ 拍馬屁

3. give a damn (about sth.) │（口語）很在乎（某事）

don't give a damn 是較粗俗、口語的表達方式，意思是「絲毫不在乎」，
因此，give a damn 就表示「很在乎」。

Bob:	I don't give a damn about the company's sales numbers!
Tommy:	You should—that's where your paycheck comes from.

鮑伯：	我才不在乎公司的銷售數字呢！
湯米：	你應該要在乎的，你的薪水就是從那裡來的。

#12 OneRepublic
Wanted

I just need to be needed. Like to know I'm crossing someone's mind.

— 〈**Wanted**〉**by OneRepublic**

我只是想被需要，想知道我正在某人的心上。

— 〈Wanted〉共和世代

適用症狀：孤單，覺得自己不重要時

副作用：自以為是職業舞者

出廠年分：2019 年

藥品屬性：流行

製造廠商：OneRepublic 共和世代

Ryan 的詞曲創作兼音樂製作人事業，幾乎跟他的樂團共和世代一樣火紅。碧昂絲、愛黛兒、魔力紅、紅髮艾德、泰勒絲（Taylor Swift）、凱莉克萊森、珍妮佛羅培茲等一拖拉庫藝人，都曾受惠於他的才華。然而，2016 年他曾一度工作到幾近過勞，開始懷疑自己是否該放棄樂團，「你開始巡迴宣傳自己的新音樂，如果它沒有紅，你就會覺得，過去這三個月都浪費了。」他曾在訪問中談到。

幸好到了該年年底，他忽然找回創作的熱情，並且寫下一首於 2019 年發表的單曲〈Rescue Me〉。這首歌曲談到了「友誼，以及是否每段友誼都值得」的真實心聲。JR 我自己感覺，這首歌很貼近共和世代最一開始的創作風格，回歸到最樸實、真實的心境。而幾個月後，他們又推出了〈Wanted〉，在這首歌裡，Ryan 赤裸裸唱出自己的心境：I just want to be someone that somebody needs. I just want to be more than a drop in the sea.「我只想當一個被需要的人，我不想要只是滄海一粟。」這種很真實、很純粹的感覺，就是共和世代！

歌曲的 MV 則很難得可以看到 Ryan 大展舞技，搭配清脆的弦樂聲以及芭蕾舞群，是聲音視覺雙重享受！

**DJ JR
歌曲
介紹時間**

▶ 歌詞中值得學習的單字片語 ◀

※ 底線單字為「複習單字」，為之前出現過的字。

1. cross one's mind | （念頭）閃現、浮現腦海中

Gina:	Has it ever crossed your mind that you might <u>be better off</u> without me?
Tommy:	What are you talking about, babe? Never in a million years.

吉娜：	你有沒有曾經想過，沒有我你可能會過得更好？
湯米：	妳在說什麼呢，寶貝？我永遠都不會那樣想。

2. a drop in the ocean/sea | 滄海一粟

Gina:	Sometimes I feel so trivial, like a drop in the ocean.
Tommy:	Well, if you could <u>read my mind</u>, you'd know you mean everything to me.

吉娜：	有時候我感到好渺小，就像是大海裡的一滴水。
湯米：	如果妳有讀心術可以看透我的內心，妳就會知道妳對我來說就是一切。

#13 Rascal Flatts
My Wish

He actually wrote it about his daughter who was graduating. And it was just so simple but said in such a nice, unique way that went so great with the melody. We knew we had to be the ones to put our voices on it.

—— Jay DeMarcus

事實上，他寫的是關於自己即將畢業的女兒，歌詞寫得極為樸實卻又如此美妙、獨特，而且跟旋律搭配得如此之好，我們聽到當下，就知道非要由我們來錄這首歌不可。

—— 樂團貝斯手傑伊

適用症狀：祝福他人，愛心氾濫時

副作用：沈浸式斷片

出廠年分：2006 年

藥品屬性：鄉村

製造廠商：Rascal Flatts 雷可福磊斯樂團

美國鄉村音樂對我們來說可能有點陌生，不過，聽聽看泰勒絲早期的創作，那就是鄉村流行音樂，而 Rascal Flatts 雷可福磊斯樂團可說是鄉村音樂的老字號樂團。伴隨著成軍二十一年的到來，他們也帶來了令人惋惜的消息，樂團將在 2020 年道別巡迴演唱之後解散。

這些年來，他們有無數歌曲攻佔排行榜，也攻佔無數死忠歌迷的心，他們翻唱的〈Bless The Broken Road〉儼然成為婚禮主題曲，佔據告示牌鄉村音樂排行榜冠軍五週，還拿下一座葛萊美獎。同樣也是翻唱的〈What Hurts The Most〉同時摘下鄉村音樂榜和成人當代音樂榜冠軍，在主流的熱門百大單曲榜也拿到第六。其中，JR 我自己最喜歡的是〈My Wish〉這首冠軍單曲。它是 2006 年由〈What Hurts The Most〉詞曲創作者原班人馬 Jeffrey Steele 和 Steve Robson 所寫的。

Jeffrey 的十三歲小女兒 Justine 一直抱怨爸爸曾經為姊姊們寫歌，卻從沒幫自己寫過，而〈My Wish〉就是在這樣的背景下誕生的。Jeffrey 提到，一開始他並沒有刻意要為孩子寫歌，但是歌詞寫著寫著就忽然發現，「這就是 Justine 的歌！我心裡想著，孩子要在一個這麼瘋狂的世界長大，我寫詞的方向是希望讓她知道，不管她做了什麼，總是會有一個人會惦記著她，總是會有一個人會在背後支持著她，不管發生什麼事。」有趣的是，錄完 demo 帶當天 Jeffrey 回到家，跟 Justine 說：「我今天幫妳寫了一首歌耶！」女兒回說：「最好是啦。」於是老爸就把歌播出來，女兒看著老爸說：「這聽起來很鄉村耶。」最後她用青少年獨有的酷酷態度說「好吧……謝啦，老爸。」老爸應該很無言吧，哈哈哈！

DJ JR
歌曲
介紹時間

▸歌詞中值得學習的單字片語 ◂

※ 底線單字為「複習單字」，為之前出現過的字。

1. When one door closes, another one opens.
上帝關了一道門，必會為你打開一扇窗。

也可以寫成 When God closes a door, He opens a window.。

Dad: I don't think we can <u>take any more chances</u>. We're down to our last penny.	爸爸：我們無法再冒任何風險了，我們只剩最後一點錢了。
Mom: When one door closes, another one opens. Don't worry. We'll <u>make it</u> through this.	媽媽：當上帝關了一道門，必定為你打開另一扇窗，不要擔心，我們會渡過難關的。

* **one's last penny** ｜最後一分錢，be down to the last penny 形容「只剩最後一點錢」。

2. come true ｜（希望或夢想）實現，成真

Mom: I can't believe we bought the house. We did it!	媽媽：我真不敢相信我們買房子了，我們做到了！
Dad: It was a struggle, but I guess dreams really do come true.	爸爸：過程真的很辛苦，不過，美夢終究還是會成真的。

#14 The Fray

How to Save a Life

I still get an incredible number of e-mails about that song. We've got friends who think it's great not having to think because they're drunk or high. But there's a better way to be happy.

—— Isaac Slade

至今我還是會收到無數關於這首歌的 e-mail，我們有些朋友覺得，借助酒精或毒品讓自己放下思慮的感覺很棒，但是，想要快樂，有比那更好的方式。

—— 主唱艾薩克

適用症狀：感到無助時，想幫助無助的人時
副作用：流淚，眼屎增多
出廠年分：2005 年
藥品屬性：流行搖滾
製造廠商：The Fray 衝突樂團

衝突樂團（The Fray）2005 年首張專輯《How To Save A Life》一推出，立馬為他們打下知名度，首支單曲〈Over My Head (Cable Car)〉描述主唱艾薩克斯雷德（Isaac Slade）跟弟弟之間的紛爭，既寫實又觸動人心，在美國境內成了榜上前十名的歌曲。緊接著第二張專輯同名單曲〈How To Save A Life〉則把他們推向了全球，在告示牌百大單曲榜擠進前三，而在英國、澳洲、加拿大、愛爾蘭、瑞典、西班牙、義大利等多個國家也進入榜上前五名。在 2000 年初，CD 開始轉為數位單曲時，這首歌跟酷玩樂團（Coldplay）的〈Viva La Vida〉是最早期的數位下載暢銷單曲。

JR 我自己認為，The Fray 的魅力在於，他們總能用細膩刻畫的敘事手法敘述生活中的平凡事物。一場夢、一次吵架、一場相遇，都成了他們筆下的題材。節奏感強烈的流行搖滾樂，搭配上柔軟的鋼琴伴奏，每一次聽歌就彷彿經歷了一次歌詞裡的故事。

〈How To Save A Life〉是有關主唱 Isaac 輔導一位染毒青少年的經歷，對方才十七歲，卻有各式各樣的人生問題，沒有人知道該怎麼幫助他。And I would have stayed up with you all night. Had I known how to save a life.（要是我知道如何拯救一條生命，我早就陪你一整夜。）副歌歌詞如此唱述，觸動了許多年輕人的內心。即使多年以後，樂團都還是會收到許多粉絲的信件，講述著自己的故事，「有個孩子死於車禍，這首歌應該是他生前所下載的最後一首歌。他們在他的葬禮上播了這首歌，有些朋友在手臂上寫上 Save A Life，人們的回應太震撼了。」Isaac 談到。

DJ JR
歌曲
介紹時間

▶歌詞中值得學習的單字片語◀

※ 底線單字為「複習單字」，為之前出現過的字。

1. stay up │熬夜

Mom: Is Charlie staying up late again?

Dad: I think he's studying for tomorrow's test. He's trying really hard to make us proud.

媽媽：查理是不是又在熬夜？

爸爸：他應該是在準備明天的考試，他很努力要讓我們感到驕傲。

2. admit to sth. │承認某事

Dad: Charlie admitted to playing online games last night when he should've been studying.

Mom: No wonder he flunked his quiz today! He's so grounded!

爸爸：查理承認他昨晚應該要讀書，但卻是在打線上遊戲。

媽媽：難怪他今天的小考不及格！他要被禁足慘了！

* **flunk** [flʌnk] *(v.)* │不及格，沒通過（考試等）

* **grounded** [ˋɡraʊndɪd] *(adj.)* │被禁足的

3. raise one's voice │（因為生氣）提高說話分貝

Jack: I don't want to hear your excuses! Why didn't you turn in the report on time?

Bob: There's no need to raise your voice. Why are you making such a big deal out of it?

傑克：我才不想聽你的藉口！你為什麼沒有準時交報告？

鮑伯：你沒必要拉高嗓音吧，幹嘛小題大作？

* **turn in** │繳交，提交，也可以寫 hand in。

* **make a big deal (out) of sth.** │小題大作，大驚小怪

適用症狀：痛苦；病痛；想幫助痛苦的朋友時

副作用：舌頭打結，結巴

出廠年分：2017 年

藥品屬性：嘻哈；饒舌

製造廠商：Lecrae ft. Tori Kelly 勒克芮 ft. 托蕾凱莉

#15 Lecrae ft. Tori Kelly

I'll Find You

Life is a precious gift. A gift we often take for granted until it is threatened. Pain can be a haunting reminder to appreciate every waking moment, so we wrote a song to share our hope in the midst of that pain.

—— Lecrae

生命是寶貴的禮物，在生命受到威脅之前，我們常將之視為理所當然。痛苦可以是一個縈繞不去的警鐘，不斷提醒著我們，要感謝每個清醒的時刻。因此，我們寫了一首歌想分享，在那痛苦之中，我們仍懷抱希望。

—— 勒克芮

基督教饒舌歌手勒克芮（Lecrae）和鐵肺歌手托蕾凱莉（Tori Kelly），風格迥異的兩人迸出了巨大的火花，〈I'll Find You〉成為兩人首支告示牌基督教音樂榜冠軍。Lecrae 在基督教饒舌音樂界是看板型人物，他本人也非常投入在社會議題上。2010 年，他寫了一首歌〈Far Away〉給海地地震災民，歌曲所有收入捐獻給救災員工。他也時常對種族議題發表演說，如 2016 年耶魯大學演講，或是在納許維爾 TEDx 發表的演說，認為嘻哈文化不該用來提倡暴力或仇視女性，而是該用來改變社會。

Tori Kelly 是《美國偶像》第九季決賽參賽者，她最讓我印象深刻的故事是，某次經紀人念她雖然很有才華，但是給大眾太無聊的形象。第二天，Tori 寫了一首歌交給經紀人，歌名叫〈Unbreakable Smile〉（擊不倒的笑容），歌詞寫著，「我不會為了多賣些唱片而穿得少一點，神把我創造得很性感，我不在乎只有我自己知道……我想改變人們的人生，給人希望，即便只是霎時片刻……」結果同名專輯衝上告示牌兩百強專輯榜第二名，完全將了經紀人一軍。

〈I'll Find You〉的靈感來自於 Lecrae 已故好友 DJ Official，也有部分受到其製作人罹患癌症的朋友影響，「在創作這首歌的時候，有一些我們心愛的人們正在對抗癌症，我們想要鼓勵他們要堅持住，想要告訴他們我們會等著、期盼著、禱告著，並且跟他們一起奮戰。」Lecrae 說道。

歌曲 MV 是在洛杉磯的格倫代爾紀念醫院拍攝，影片有數名癌症病童參與在其中，非常感人！

DJ JR
歌曲
介紹時間

▸ 歌詞中值得學習的單字片語 ◂

1. turn to sb. ｜向某人求助

字面意義是「轉向某人」，意思就是「求助於、請求支援於某人」。

2. hold on ｜堅持，撐住

hold on 有「等一下」、「抓住某物（hold on to sth.）」、「堅持、撐住」的意思。
歌詞裡是後者，叫人在痛苦中要堅持住。

3. hang (on) by a thread ｜岌岌可危；命懸一線

Bob:	My career is hanging by a thread. I shouldn't have gotten on Jack's bad side.	鮑伯：我的工作岌岌可危了，我不應該惹毛傑克的。
Tommy:	Don't mind him. Next time he gives you trouble, you know who to turn to.	湯米：別理會他，下次他找你麻煩，你就知道可以找誰了。

* **get on one's bad side** ｜得罪某人，把某人惹火
* **give sb. trouble** ｜找某人麻煩；給某人製造麻煩

4. go through ｜經歷（困難或讓人沮喪的事）

I know you're going through a rough time, but don't worry. Things will get better in no time.
我知道你正在經歷艱難的時刻，不過不要擔心。事情很快會好轉。

* **in no time** ｜很快，馬上

適用症狀：失去親愛的家人時
副作用：淚流不止
出廠年分：2017 年
藥品屬性：流行
製造廠商：Ed Sheeran 紅髮艾德

#16 Ed Sheeran

Supermarket Flowers

I just wanted to make a tribute to my gran. She was the musical one in my family. Hopefully I will pass that on to my kids.

—— **Ed Sheeran**

我只想向我的祖母致敬，她是家族裡最有音樂細胞的一位，希望有一天，我也可以將這個天分傳給我的孩子。

—— 紅髮艾德

愛爾蘭籍的安妮是紅髮艾德（Ed Sheeran）的祖母，她也是啟發馬修和艾德兄弟倆追求音樂事業的恩人。艾德提及安妮時曾說：「她是家族裡最有音樂細胞的一位，希望有一天，我也可以把這個天賦傳給我的孩子。」

這首歌是為了紀念已經離世的安妮。安妮過世當天，艾德跟家人到醫院裡清空病房，艾德正在收拾窗臺上超市買來的鮮花，就在那麼一刻，觸動了艾德寫下這首動人歌曲的靈感。在安妮的葬禮上，祖父比爾轉過身來對艾德說：「你一定要把那首歌放到專輯裡，那回憶太美麗了……。」

這並非艾德第一次寫下關於祖父母的歌，先前的〈Nancy Mulligan〉寫的是祖父母相遇的故事，〈Afire Love〉寫的則是罹患阿茲海默症二十年過世的祖父，而這首〈Supermarket Flowers〉則是為了紀念祖母安妮而創作的感傷、美麗、令人起雞皮疙瘩的歌曲。

2019 年一項調查裡，〈Supermarket Flowers〉是英國喪禮上最常播放的歌曲第六名，至於第一名是哪一首呢？就是我們在第一首歌提到的，法蘭克辛納屈的〈My Way〉。

DJ JR 歌曲介紹時間

▶ 歌詞中值得學習的單字片語 ◀

※ 底線單字為「複習單字」，為之前出現過的字。

1. pack up｜打包；收拾行李

Gina:	I'm packing up and leaving you for good!	吉娜：我要收拾行李，永遠離開你。
Tommy:	Why? Whatever I may have done, I promise I'll <u>make it right</u>.	湯米：為什麼？無論我可能做了什麼，我答應妳我會改正的。
Gina:	Happy April Fools' Day!	吉娜：愚人節快樂！
Tommy:	...	湯米：……

2. be/feel down｜不開心；沮喪

Jenny:	I've been feeling so down lately. I can't work, can't sleep, can't seem to <u>keep it together</u>.	珍妮：我最近感覺好糟喔，無法工作，無法睡覺，沒辦法振作精神。
Gina:	Cheer up, girl. You wanna go shopping after work today?	吉娜：女孩，開心點，下班後要一起去血拼嗎？
Jenny:	I'm down!	珍妮：我要！

* **I'm down.**｜在例句裡是個雙關語，一方面有「我很沮喪」的意思；
另一方面，當別人提議或給建議時，本人回答 I'm down. 就表示
「（同意）我要去、我要做、我要吃」等等。

#17 Lukas Graham

Here (For Christmas)

This is about William, my childhood friend, who is no longer with us. He was renovating this beautiful old boat, but he never got to put it in the water. That boat is a metaphor for all the things I wish I could do with Willy, my dad and all the others that are here no more.

—— Lukas Forchhammer

這首歌是關於我已經不在的童年好友威廉，他曾經整修一艘漂亮的舊船，但他沒有機會讓它下水。那艘船象徵著所有我盼望能跟威廉、我爸以及那些不在的人一起做的事。

—— 主唱盧卡斯

製造廠商：Lukas Graham 盧卡斯葛拉漢樂團
藥品屬性：佳節
出廠年分：2019 年
副作用：又哭又笑；聲帶肌肉拉傷
適用症狀：懷念已故的朋友

盧卡斯葛拉漢樂團（Lukas Graham）是 2011 年成立的丹麥三人樂團，第一張專輯僅在歐洲發行，立馬搶佔丹麥專輯榜首位。2015 年，一般他們稱之為「藍色專輯」的第二張同名專輯則打入了國際市場，特別是單曲〈7 Years〉，這也是讓 JR 我第一次注意到這個團體的歌，它在丹麥、義大利、奧地利、比利時和瑞典都登頂榜單。接著，他們在美國各大脫口秀上的現場表演，引起北美圈的注意，〈7 Years〉在 Spotify 的串流次數也迅速竄升到前幾名，直到 2016 年專輯才正式在美國發行，到該年年底〈7 Years〉被提名了三項葛萊美獎，雖然很可惜沒有拿獎，但是自此，Lukas Graham 就已經奠定了樂壇上的地位。

除了〈7 Years〉，我也非常喜歡紀念他父親的〈You're Not There〉、他跟交往已久女友之間感情的〈Love Someone〉、〈Lie〉等，其中〈Here (For Christmas)〉則是一首聖誕單曲，光是聽歌曲前幾秒的旋律，就有種濃濃的「聖誕節來了」的感覺。不過在溫馨溫暖的旋律背後，講述的卻是主唱盧卡斯福特漢默（Lukas Forchhammer）對 2018 年過世老友的思念，每到這個季節，無法不想起他，不知道是該哭還是會心一笑，Gone don't always mean that you disappear. 'Cause inside all of us you're still here.（離開不總是代表消逝無蹤，因為在我們內心中，你仍與我們同在）；歌曲 MV 裡盡都是 Lukas 跟好友 William 從小到大一起生活的照片和畫面，既溫馨又帶有濃濃的洋蔥味。

DJ JR 歌曲介紹時間

▶ 歌詞中值得學習的單字片語 ◀

※ 底線單字為「複習單字」，為之前出現過的字。

1. pick out │ 挑選出

Jack: It just <u>crossed my mind</u> that we should pick out a few samples for the client before the meeting.

Jenny: Do you want me to bring you all the samples, or should I just pick some out myself?

傑克：我突然想到，我們應該在會議前事先挑出一些樣品給客戶。

珍妮：你要我把樣品都帶來給你看，還是我自己挑一些就可以了？

2. like hell │（口語）非常地，極度地

近似於 like crazy；也可以當作「不同意」的口語說法，但是用起來可是相當不禮貌的喔！

(on the phone)

Gina: We all miss you like hell. When are you gonna come visit us?

Amy: I can book a flight and <u>pack up</u> <u>in no time</u>.

（電話上）

吉娜：我們都想死妳了，妳什麼時候過來拜訪我們啊？

艾咪：我可以立馬訂機票收拾行李。

Gina: Amy's coming to stay with us for a couple days next week.

Tommy: Like hell she is! Last time she was here, she <u>turned</u> our house <u>into</u> a nightclub.

Gina: Come on. It wasn't that bad.

吉娜：艾咪下禮拜要過來我們這邊住幾天。

湯米：她最好是！上次她來，她簡直把我們家變成了夜店。

吉娜：別這樣嘛，也沒那麼糟啦。

#18 Alessia Cara

Rooting For You

It's like watching a movie and you see the protagonist go the wrong way and you're instantly like, "Dude, no. I was rooting for you. Why you got to go and do that?"

—— **Alessia Cara**

就像是在看電影時，你看到主角走上錯誤的道路，然後你瞬間心想「老兄，不！我一直在幫你加油耶，你為什麼非得要這麼做？」

—— 艾莉西亞卡拉

適用症狀：遇到忘恩負義的朋友；熱臉貼冷屁股

副作用：滄海三聲苦笑，哈！哈！哈！

出廠年分：2019 年

藥品屬性：流行

製造廠商：Alessia Cara 艾莉西亞卡拉

許多人是從 2016 年迪士尼電影《海洋奇緣》（*Moana*）開始知道加拿大籍的艾莉希亞卡拉（Alessia Cara），沒錯！她就是電影原聲帶中〈How Far I'll Go〉的原唱，畫面有拼湊起來了嗎？但是其實她在 2014 年就已經出道，首支單曲〈Here〉在沒有大筆行銷預算投入的情況之下，竟然表現得出奇地好，一度上到告示牌百大單曲榜第五名，之後一連串單曲都獲得不錯好評，像是〈Scars To Your Beautiful〉、〈Trust My Lonely〉、跟 Zedd 合作的〈Stay〉、〈October〉等；Alessia 在 2018 年獲得葛萊美最佳新人獎，許多人認為她跟已故知名歌手艾美懷絲（Amy Winehouse）歌聲很神似，確實有相似之處！

我喜歡描述巡演時跟好友共處的〈October〉的懷舊唱腔與旋律，也很喜歡邊抱怨朋友邊調侃自己的〈Rooting For You〉。〈Rooting For You〉這首歌描述自己因朋友的冷漠而感到心冷：Why you gotta be so cold in the summertime? I was really rooting for ya.（你為什麼非得在炎炎夏日表現得這麼冷漠？虧我還幫你加油打氣。）我想，這種情況多數人都經歷過，正所謂熱臉貼冷屁股，加上旋律和節奏有種淘氣的感覺，聆聽時真像是苦中作樂啊。在 Jimmy Fallon 的脫口秀上，Alessia 還提到她曾在實境節目《America's Next Top Model》（超級名模生死鬥）上看到一個片段，是主持人泰拉班克斯（Tyra Banks）破口大罵其中一個不受教的參賽者：I was rooting for you. We were all rooting for you! How dare you!（我一直在幫妳加油，我們都在幫妳加油！妳怎敢這麼說！）Alessia 原本想把這個片段收錄在單曲裡，結果因聯絡不上 Tyra 團隊只得作罷。

DJ JR 歌曲介紹時間

▶ 歌詞中值得學習的單字片語 ◀

1. elephant in the room｜（不願提及的）棘手問題

如果說「在房間裡有大象（elephant）」，表示有一個顯而易見的問題或是困難情況，
麻煩或尷尬到讓人不願去面對或談論。

Jenny: The fact that the project is way over budget is really an elephant in the room.

Bob: <u>Tell me about it</u>, somebody should <u>call Jack out</u> for overspending on the project.

珍妮：專案預算超支的問題真的很尷尬。

鮑伯：這還用說，應該要有人指出傑克專案超支這件事。

2. be tired of sb./sth.｜厭倦了某人事物

3. root for sb./sth.｜幫某人或某事打氣加油

Jenny: I've been working so hard for this promotion. I really hope I get it.

Gina: Everybody thinks you deserve it, Jenny. We're all rooting for you!

珍妮：我為了這次升遷真的很努力工作，我真的很希望可以拿到。

吉娜：大家都覺得那是妳應得的，珍妮，我們都在幫妳加油！

* **promotion** [prə`moʃən] *(n.)*｜升遷，也有「促銷活動」的意思。

4. burn one's bridges｜自斷退路

Dad: I'd be burning my bridges with the company if I switch jobs now.

Mom: But if they're willing to give you a higher salary, maybe you should <u>take a chance</u>.

爸爸：如果我現在換工作，就真的跟公司鬧翻了。

媽媽：可是如果他們願意給你較高的薪水，也許你應該賭賭看。

#19 Oh Wonder
Happy

適用症狀：遇見前任男女朋友；真心祝福前任時

副作用：情緒錯亂性內分泌失調；又「苦」又笑

出廠年分：2020 年

藥品屬性：另類流行

製造廠商：Oh Wonder 汪德雙人組

I'd seen a picture of my ex-girlfriend that morning getting married and I never thought... Well, I never thought I'd be happy. I had that exact feeling, I was just buzzing. That's so cool she found someone she loves.

—— Anthony West

有天早上，我看見前女友結婚的照片，我從沒想過……嗯，我沒想過我會發自內心感到開心，我心中確實感到開心，那感覺充斥我心頭，她能找到真愛實在是太酷的一件事了。

—— 安東尼衛斯特

汪德雙人組（Oh Wonder）是英國約瑟芬范德古赫特（Josephine Vander Gucht）和安東尼衛斯特（Anthony West）組成的獨立音樂團體，他們獨特的風格真的很不主流，一開始 JR 我聽得有點不習慣，但是聽久了，他們樸實、正能量的曲風、歌詞會漸漸地讓你喜歡上他們。

Oh Wonder 所有歌曲都是由約瑟芬和安東尼自行創作，直到 2020 年最新專輯《No One Else Can Wear Your Crown》，首度邀請其他詞曲作家合作，「當你習慣了一個人把鋼琴搬上廂型車後座，然後開車到格拉斯格市表演，突然讓其他人進入變得有點困難……感覺我們就像是一個新的樂團一般。」約瑟芬接受採訪時談到。新專輯裡大談友誼、親情、安慰、支持、夢想、見到前情人的心情等，〈Happy〉就是講述遇到前情人的心境，I never thought I'd be happy to see you with somebody new. Never thought I'd be happy to see you do the things we do.（我從沒想過會開心見到你跟另一個人在一起，從沒想過我會開心見到你跟別人做那些我們以前一起做的事），聽的時候有種內心洗三溫暖的感覺，澀中帶甜的滋味，難以形容，趕快自己聽聽看吧！

DJ JR 歌曲 介紹時間

019

▶ 歌詞中值得學習的單字片語 ◀

1. let sb. go/let go of sb. ｜讓某人自由

「放開某人」的意思，也可以當作「讓某人自由」。

It's really hard to let go of someone you've truly loved.
對於你曾經真心愛過的人，要放手真的很難。

....

2. call it/things even ｜（口語）扯平了

Gina:	Did you forget to mow the lawn?	吉娜：你是不是忘了割草坪？
Tommy:	Um... well you forgot to do the dishes. How about we call it even?	湯米：嗯⋯⋯妳不也忘了洗碗盤，這樣是不是算扯平了？
Gina:	You wish!	吉娜：你想得美！

* **do the dishes** ｜洗碗盤，等同於 wash the dishes

* **You wish!** ｜（口語）想得美！

#20 Ed Sheeran ft. Khalid

Beautiful People

The tune is about remaining true to yourself and not trying to become one of those so-called "beautiful people" obsessed with material things and stature.

—— *Rolling Stone*

這首歌是關於忠於自我，不汲汲營營於變成那些沉迷於追求物質名利的所謂「上流人士」。

——《滾石雜誌》

適用症狀：邊緣人；覺得自己格格不入

副作用：無欲無求，六根清淨

出廠年分：2019 年

藥品屬性：流行

製造廠商：Ed Sheeran ft. Khalid 紅髮艾德 ft. 凱利德

〈Beautiful People〉的 MV 2019 年 6 月一上傳 YouTube，我就立馬點開來看，看到泳池派對、身材火辣的名模在跳舞，瞬間我心想「艾德什麼時候開始做起派對音樂了？」原來誤會大了，因為剛好相反地，這首歌是在反諷五光四射、金光閃閃的上流社會；從歌名開始講起，〈Beautiful People〉（字面意思：美麗的人）一詞在六〇年代常常是用來嘲諷那些有權、有錢、有勢的人們，著名的披頭四一曲〈Baby You're A Rich Man〉裡就有唱到 How does it feel to be one of the beautiful people?（身為上流人士感覺如何？），而〈Beautiful People〉的 MV 其實是在刻畫一對平凡的夫妻試著要融入卻無法融入上流社會的寫實模樣，這也反映出艾德和凱利德（Khalid）的真實心境，如果仔細看，在其中幾幕還可以看到兩個人客串在那群「美麗人們」當中。

〈Beautiful People〉成為紅髮艾德第四張專輯中的第二支英國單曲排行榜冠軍，第一支是跟小賈斯汀（Justin Bieber）合作的〈I Don't Care〉，其實這兩首歌裡都可以聽得出艾德很樸實、不習慣所謂的「名人派對生活」，誠如歌詞所唱的 We don't fit in well 'cause we are just ourselves. I could use some help getting out of this conversation.（我們顯得很突兀，因為我們就是自己真實的模樣，能不能幫幫我從這段對話中抽身？）

DJ JR 歌曲介紹時間

020

▶ 歌詞中值得學習的單字片語 ◀

1. figure out │ 搞懂、搞清楚

Jenny: The printer isn't working, but I can't figure out what's wrong with it.

Bob: Let me take a look. OK, I figured out what the problem is—there's a paper jam.

珍妮：印表機不能用了，可是我搞不清楚問題在哪裡。

鮑伯：我來看一下。好，我找到問題了，它卡紙了啦。

2. fit in │ 融入或適應某環境、團體等

Jack: Hey, Tommy. Let's get out of here. I don't fit in at this party.

Tommy: I can't figure you out. I thought you liked parties.

傑克：嘿，湯米，我們走吧，我有點無法融入這派對。

湯米：我搞不懂你耶，我以為你喜歡派對。

Inspirational Stories

正 能 量 文 章

PART 2

正能量
座右銘
MOTTO

I don't judge my self-worth as a football player. Football is something I love. It's a fun career deal, but it's not what I want to do with my life because I see football as a game.

我不會用美式足球員的身分來評價我的自我價值。美式足球是我熱愛的事，是個有趣的職業，但並不是我人生的全部，因為對我來說，美式足球就是個比賽。

—— NFL 前紐約噴射機隊明星四分衛
Tim Tebow 提姆提伯

The Making of

一個 ▶ YouTuber 的誕生

Soy Jessi, a young YouTube star, experienced a huge loss of views after she took a break from the [1]**platform**. Her mother had [2]**passed away**, and so she [3]**took some time off**. She came back a few months later, but the views didn't. Maybe that's what happens when you stop feeding the [4]**notorious** ❶**algorithm**. Or maybe that's just what happens when your [5]**audience** [6]**moves on**.

It's every social media ❷**influencer**'s challenge to stay [7]**relevant** in the online world. But what is the key factor to having this social media [8]**clout**? Is it really all about the algorithm game? Or does quality [9]**content** [10]**count**?

In his videos, Casey Neistat has repeatedly [11]**brought up** his [12]**big break** on YouTube. After making videos on the platform for five years, he decided to do daily ❸**vlogging**. In a couple of weeks, his channel [13]**exploded**. People started noticing his stuff.

So hate it, but admit it. The algorithm [14]**definitely** [15]**plays a role in** your online success. That's why YouTubers are [16]**stepping up their game**, [17]**cranking new videos out** with greater and greater [18]**frequency**. In fact, one of the fastest growing Taiwanese YouTubers, Saint（聖結石）, [19]**came to fame** by uploading daily within the first nine months.

However, you could be doing all the right things—have a crazy uploading schedule, make [20]**eye-catching** ❹**thumbnails**, write [21]**appealing** titles, even ❺**clickbaity** ones—but still not get it right. Viewers won't ❻**subscribe** if they don't find value in your content,

a YouTuber

021

#01

whether it be entertainment, knowledge, a sense of ²²**company** or anything else. It's the algorithm, the thumbnails, the titles that ²³**draw** the audience in, but it's the content that makes them stay. No single element stands alone—they all ²⁴**go hand in hand**.

※ 底線單字為「複習單字」，為之前出現過的字。

❺ clickbaity

騙點閱的，當形容詞。名詞是 clickbait「騙點閱的圖文或影片」，由 click（點擊）＋ bait（誘餌）而來。

．．．．．．．．．．．．．．．．．．．．．．．．．．．．

❻ subscribe/ unsubscribe

訂閱／取消訂閱，在 YouTube 上叫人訂閱就用這個字。在 Facebook fan page 和 Instagram 上，則是用 follow/unfollow「追蹤／取消追蹤」。subscriber 則是「訂閱者、訂閱用戶」。

JR YouTube 影片 #3

很多人都知道，演算法對於 YouTuber 來說非常重要，也知道，影片要下個好標題、放個精緻的縮圖才會吸引人觀看。然而即便如此，這也絕不是高觀看次數的票房保證，它就像是產品的包裝、促銷，可以吸引人購買，但是一支影片真正的價值取決於產品本身──內容，影片是否引起觀眾的共鳴，是否帶給觀眾價值。我們個人也是如此，外在的面貌、穿著、頭銜、魅力、話術很吸引人，然而，身為人最大的價值是內在的「你自己的品行」。

JR的話

The Making of
a YouTuber

一個 YouTuber
的誕生

Soy Jessi 是位年紀很小的 YouTube 明星,她暫離平臺休息一段時間之後,觀看次數便大幅減少。她的母親過世了,於是她休息一段時間。幾個月後她回來了,可是觀看數字卻回不來了。當你停止餵食那惡名昭彰的演算法時,也許就會發生這種事,又或許單純只是觀眾找到新對象了。

每一位網紅都努力在網路世界裡保持能見度,但是保有這社群媒體影響力的關鍵要素究竟是什麼?真的只是在玩這場演算法遊戲嗎?還是產出有品質的內容也很重要?

Casey Neistat 在幾部自己的影片中,曾反覆提到他在 YouTube 崛起的契機。當時他已經在 YouTube 做了五年影片,接著他決定改做每日影片。在幾個禮拜之內,他的頻道就迅速爆紅,人們開始注意到他的作品。

所以儘管恨得牙癢癢的,但我們不得不承認,演算法對於在網路上取得成功有一定影響,這就是為什麼 YouTuber 們得不斷更上一層樓,不顧一切提升每週發片的頻率,事實上,其中一位成長速度最快的臺灣 YouTuber —— 聖結石,就是因為在前九個月每日發片而迅速竄紅。

然而,就算你做了所有對的事情 —— 固定發片、用吸睛縮圖、吸引人的標題、甚至是騙點閱的標題,還是有可能白搭。觀眾如果無法在你的作品中找到價值,他們就不會訂閱你的頻道,不管那是娛樂型頻道、知識型、陪伴型或其他類型頻道。儘管演算法、縮圖、標題可以把觀眾吸引進來,然而,讓他們決定留下來的是內容。沒有哪個元素是特別重要,全都是相輔相成的。

Vocabulary & Phrases
單字片語

※ 底線單字為「複習單字」，為之前出現過的字。

---

1. platform [ˋplæt͵fɔrm] *(n.)* │（實質或形式上的）平臺；月臺

There's a wooden platform in the middle of the park where performances are held.
在公園中央有個供人表演的木質平臺。

YouTube is a great platform for sharing videos.
YouTube 是分享影片的絕佳平臺。

---

2. pass away │（委婉說法）過世

My grandmother passed away in the hospital on March 16th.
我的外婆三月十六日在醫院過世了。

---

3. take time off │請假；抽出時間

I took some time off from work to decompress.
我從工作中抽出時間讓自己恢復精神。

* decompress [͵dikəmˋprɛs] *(v.)* │減壓，放鬆

---

4. notorious [noˋtorɪəs] *(adj.)* │惡名昭彰的

Jack is notorious for bossing people around.
傑克是出了名喜歡對別人頤指氣使。

---

5. audience [ˋɔdɪəns] *(n.)* │觀眾，聽眾

The audience was all ears throughout the speech.
聽眾聚精會神聆聽整場演講。

PART 2 │ 正能量文章 │ *What's Going on Around the World?* **061**

6. move on │ 轉換到新階段；接受現實繼續前進

Tommy was having a hard time moving on after he broke up with his ex.
湯米跟前女友分手後，一直走出不出來。

* have a hard time (doing sth.) │ 做某件事遇到困難或不好的經驗

....

7. relevant [ˋrɛləvənt] *(adj.)* │ 有意義的，關係重大的；切題的

Social media influencers are doing more and more extreme things to remain relevant to audiences.
網紅做越來越多極端的事情，只為了維持人氣。

....

8. clout [klaut] *(n.)* │ 權勢；影響力

We're living in an era where influencers can have more clout than the mainstream media.
我們活在一個網紅可以比主流媒體擁有更大影響力的時代。

....

9. content [ˋkɑntənt] *(n.)* │ 內容

The increase in clickbaity titles and off-the-wall content is partially a result of the YouTube algorithm.
騙點閱的標題和古怪的內容越來越多，部分是受到 YouTube 演算法所致。

* off-the-wall [ˋɔfðəˋwɔl] *(adj.)* │ 驚人的，不同尋常的

....

10. count [kaunt] *(v.)* │ 認為，看作；算數

I count myself lucky to have such a supportive family.
我自認幸運能擁有一個很支持我的家庭。

You cheated. That doesn't count!
你作弊，不算！

....

11. bring up (sb./sth.) │ 提到、談起（某人某事）

Don't ever bring up Tommy's ex with him, especially when Gina's around.
千萬別在湯米面前提起前任，特別是吉娜在旁邊的時候。

12. big break │ 大好機會；機緣

Jenny got her big break when she won a part in a Hollywood movie.
珍妮得到大好機會，贏得演出一部好萊塢電影的角色。

13. explode [ɪk`splod] *(v.)* │ 激增，爆炸性成長

Sales have exploded since the company decided to target a younger generation of consumers.
自從公司決定轉向年輕消費者族群之後，銷售數字便呈爆炸性成長。

14. definitely [`dɛfənɪtli] *(adv.)* │ 當然，毫無疑問

Tommy is definitely afraid to talk about Susan in front of Gina.
湯米絕對不敢在吉娜面前講到蘇珊。

15. play a (key/major/important) role in sth. │ 在某事扮演（關鍵／重大／重要）角色

Jenny has played an important role in the project's success.
專案之所以能成功，珍妮絕對扮演了很重要的角色。

16. (step) up one's game │ 提升表現水準

You need to step up your game if you wanna compete with the big YouTube creators.
如果你想要跟那些大咖 YouTube 創作者競爭，你就必須得加把勁才行。

17. crank out │ 大量且快速產出

指不需什麼思考，草草快速完成大量事情。

Stephen King is famous for cranking out new novels year after year.
史蒂芬金是出了名一年接一年大量出書。

18. frequency [`frikwənsi] *(n.)* │ 頻率，次數

I've found that cranking out videos to sustain a certain upload frequency isn't necessarily a key factor to success.
我發現，為了維持上傳影片頻率而大量產出影片，不見得是成功的關鍵要素。

* sustain [sə`sten] *(v.)* │ 維持，持續

19. come/rise to fame ｜成名

He rose to fame by making goofy videos of him <u>making fun of</u> himself.
他靠著拍攝搞笑自嘲影片而成名。

* **goofy** [`gufi] *(adj.)* ｜（口語）愚蠢的；滑稽的

....

20. eye-catching [`aɪ.kætʃɪŋ] *(adj.)* ｜吸睛的，引人注目的

Jenny's neon yellow dress is so eye-catching!
珍妮的螢光黃裙子實在有夠吸睛！

....

21. appealing [ə`pilɪŋ] *(adj.)* ｜有吸引力的；令人感興趣的

Jenny has an appealing personality.
珍妮有著吸引人的個性。

The idea of working from home is quite appealing.
在家工作這點子挺吸引人的。

....

22. company [`kʌmpənɪ] *(n.)* ｜作伴，陪伴

If you enjoy Gina's company so much, you should ask her to marry you.
如果你這麼喜愛吉娜的陪伴，你就該向她求婚。

....

23. draw [drɔ] *(v.)* ｜吸引，招來

The famous university draws students from all over the world.
這所知名大學吸引來自全世界各地的學生前來就讀。

....

24. go hand in hand (with sth.) ｜（與某事）密切相關

hand in hand 是手牽手，延伸為「與……密切相關」的意思。

High-quality lenses and large sensors go hand in hand with sharp photos.
要拍出高畫質的照片，高品質鏡頭和大感光元件是密切相關的。

It was taking over my life, and I was becoming obsessed by it. Like, 'How many likes did I get?' and 'What did people say about my picture?' and who's doing this and who's doing that. I found myself focusing more on my Instagram life than I was on my real life.

它佔據了我的生活，我變得太過沉迷於其中，像是「有多少人按讚？」「人們對我的照片發表了什麼看法？」還有誰在做這個、誰在做那個。我發現我花在 Instagram 上的心力，比花在真實人生上的還要多。

——《蜘蛛人》演員
Tom Holland 湯姆荷蘭

Why Are Social Me Networks Hiding T

❶ anxiety

焦慮，不安。它也是「焦慮症」的醫學名詞；**anxious** 則是形容詞「焦慮的」。

....

❷ depression

憂鬱，抑鬱。在醫學上則是指「憂鬱症」。**depressed** 則是形容詞，說自己 **I'm so depressed.** 不代表我有憂鬱症喔！而是說「我好鬱卒喔。」

....

❸ FOMO

fear of missing out 的縮寫，以中文來說就是「害怕錯過（精采的事情）」，這是社群媒體時代下所產生的新名詞，形容人們因害怕在社群上錯過消息而變得焦慮。

....

❹ body image

身體意象。指一個人對自己身體的看法、信念和情感態度，身體意象會受到社會文化認知的影響，負面的身體意象更常發生在女性身上，如擔心自己的身材不符合當下價值。

From Yahoo and Facebook to Instagram and Line, the means of online communication have steadily ¹**evolved**. Essentially, these platforms exist to provide us with a sense of connection and belonging. But we've been hearing the ²**opposite** more in recent days—people feeling disconnected as a result of being on social media.

A 2017 *Time* magazine article titled, "Why Instagram Is the Worst Social Media for Mental Health" ³**quoted** data from a survey that associated the social media platform with high levels of ❶**anxiety**, ❷**depression**, ⁴**bullying** and ❸**FOMO**. And it wasn't just Instagram. YouTube, Facebook, Twitter, Snapchat and Instagram all received negative marks for sleep quality, bullying and ❹**body image**.

Selena Gomez, who once had the most followers on Instagram, has taken a break from the app several times to ⁵**improve** her ❺**mental health**. She said it became ⁶**addictive** and that she was constantly seeing things she didn't want to see, thinking about things that she didn't want to care about. ⁷**In her own words**, "I always ⁸**end up** feeling like shit when I look at Instagram."

So how are corporations ⁹**coping with** this worrying trend? Instagram has been ¹⁰**experimenting** with a new app ¹¹**interface** that hides the number of likes photos get. "We want people to worry a little bit less about how many likes they're getting on Instagram and spend a bit more time connecting with the people that they care about," said Instagram CEO Adam Mosseri. And just in case you haven't noticed, the follower count was previously moved to a less obvious place and ¹²**reduced** to a smaller font.

為什麼社群媒體要隱藏數字？

...ir Numbers?

Twitter CEO Jack Dorsey mentioned at a TED [13]**forum** in early 2019 that if he were to [14]**redesign** Twitter, he'd [15]**leave out** the "like" [16]**feature**. And YouTube has stopped showing full <u>subscriber</u> counts, instead displaying [17]**abbreviated** [18]**figures** like 1.6k, 117k, 52m, etc. Some have [19]**speculated** that the purpose was to keep YouTubers from [20]**obsessing over** sub counts so much.

All in all, I think using social media is fine as long as we focus more on real life—having face-to-face [21]**interactions** with people and living in the present moment. It's nice to share your life online once in a while when you feel like it. But things start [22]**going downhill** when you get too [20]**obsessed with** the numbers. I think that for both social media companies and users, maybe it's just time to go back to when everything was simpler.

※ 底線單字為「複習單字」，為之前出現過的字。

❺ mental health

心理健康，相對地，「身體健康」就是 physical health，不過，一般說 healthy（健康）就是指身體健康啦。如果要強調心理或是身體上的健康，就可以說 She is mentally healthy./She is physically healthy. 相反則可以說 mentally ill 和 physically ill。

JR YouTube
影片 #4

JR的話

有時候，我還挺懷念沒有社群媒體的年代，但又無法否認它所帶來的便利性。社群媒體在帶給我們無比便利的同時，是不是也讓我們失去了一點生活品質呢？該如何在溝通的質與量之間找到平衡點？我想，答案唯有存在於「個人意志力」了。

Why Are Social Media Networks Hiding Their Numbers?

為什麼社群媒體
要隱藏數字？

從雅虎、臉書到 Instagram、Line，線上溝通的方式不斷地在進化當中。本質上來講，這些平臺存在的目的是為提供連結與歸屬感，但最近，我們卻更常聽到截然相反的聲音 —— 使用社群媒體讓人們更加疏離。

《時代雜誌》2017 年一篇標題為〈為什麼 Instagram 是對心理健康最有害的社群媒體〉的文章，引用了一項調查資料，提到社群媒體跟焦慮、憂慮、霸凌和社群媒體恐慌呈現高度相關。而且不只是在 Instagram。YouTube、臉書、推特、Snapchat 和 Instagram 在睡眠品質、霸凌與身體意象所得到的分數也很低。

席琳娜戈梅茲曾經是 Instagram 上最多人追蹤的人，她過去曾為了改善心理健康，好幾次停用這個應用程式。她說她變得對 Instagram 上癮，總是不停看著她根本不想看的東西，想著她根本不想在乎的事。套句她自己說的話：「我每次刷 Instagram 的時候，心情總是糟透了。」

所以，各企業要如何因應這個令人憂心的趨勢呢？Instagram 正在開發新介面，將圖片按讚數隱藏起來。Instagram 執行長亞當莫塞里說：「我們希望人們少去擔心自己得到多少讚，花多點時間跟他們所在乎的人連繫。」還有，怕你沒注意到，先前追蹤數也被移到一個比較不明顯的地方，字體也變小了。

推特執行長傑克多西則在 2019 年初的 TED 論壇上提到，如果他可以重新設計推特，他會移除按讚功能。YouTube 則是已經停止顯示完整的頻道訂閱數字，改用簡化的數字呈現，如 1.6k、117k、52m 等。有些人推測，其用意是要淡化 YouTuber 們之間著魔似的訂閱數比較。

總之，我覺得使用社群媒體這件事本身完全沒問題，只要我們更用心在自己的現實生活上 —— 面對面的互動，並且活在當下。當你心血來潮，偶爾在網路上跟人分享生活也挺不錯的。不過，當你對數字過於沉迷的時候，情況就會開始走下坡。對於社群媒體企業和使用者兩方面來說，現在也許正是反璞歸真的時候。

Vocabulary & Phrases
單字片語

※ 底線單字為「複習單字」，為之前出現過的字。

1. evolve [ɪˋvɑlv] (v.) │ 進化，逐步發展

Over the past century, communication devices have evolved from huge boxes hanging on the wall to smartphones that you can put in your pocket.
在過去一個世紀，通訊設備從掛在牆上的巨大箱子，演變成小到可以放在口袋裡的智慧型手機。

2. opposite [ˋɑpəzɪt] (adj.) │ 相反的，對立的

You're going in the opposite direction. The stadium is that way!
你完全走反方向了，體育場在那個方向！

3. quote [kwot] (v.) │ 引用，引述，援引

JR likes to quote successful people in his speeches.
JR 喜歡在演講中引用成功人士的話。

4. bully [ˋbʊli] (v.)/(n.) │ 霸凌；霸凌者

「霸凌」的意思，作為名詞時是「霸凌者，以大欺小的人」，至於「霸凌行為」則說 bullying。

JR was a short kid who got bullied at school. Luckily, he didn't grow up to become a bully himself.
JR 小時候個子很矮，所以常在學校被霸凌，幸好他長大後沒有成為會霸凌別人的人。

5. improve [ɪmˋpruv] (v.) │ 改進，改善

To quote *National Geographic* editor Bob Gilka, "You don't have to prove yourself, not to me, or to the other photographers. What I do demand that you do is improve yourself."
引用《國家地理雜誌》前總編輯鮑伯吉爾卡的話 —— 「你不用向我或是其他攝影師證明自己。我要你做的是，不斷改進自己。」

6. addictive [əˋdɪktɪv] *(adj.)* │ **使人上癮的**

而 addicted 則是「上癮的」。

Online games are so addictive they can make you <u>stay up</u> all night playing them.
線上遊戲非常容易上癮，會讓你熬夜玩一整晚。

Charlie is addicted to video games.
查理對電動上癮。

7. in one's (own) words │ **用自己的話說**

Please tell us in your own words what you saw on the night of the murder.
請用你自己的話告訴我們，你在兇殺案當晚看到了什麼。

8. end up │ **最終成為；最後處於**

Charlie ended up being <u>grounded</u> and <u>doing the dishes</u> for a month after he was caught playing online games in the middle of the night.
查理半夜偷玩線上遊戲被抓包，最後淪落到被禁足和洗碗盤一整個月。

9. cope (with sth.) │ **應付；妥善處理**

Paul plays video games to cope with the stress of his high-pressure job.
保羅藉由打電動來紓解沉重的工作壓力。

Alan <u>had a hard time</u> coping with the heartbreak of his divorce.
離婚所帶來的心痛讓亞倫難以招架。

10. experiment [ɪkˋspɛrəmənt] *(v.)* │ **進行實驗；嘗試新事物**

Jack and Bob are experimenting with all kinds of different ideas for the new marketing campaign.
傑克和鮑伯為了新的行銷活動，正在嘗試各種新點子。

11. interface [ˋɪntəˌfes] *(n.)* │ **介面**

The new website interface sucks!
新的網站介面爛透了！

12. reduce [rɪ`djus] (v.) | 減少，降低

The budget for Jack and Bob's project has been reduced by thirty percent.
傑克和鮑伯的專案預算被刪了百分之三十。

13. forum [`forəm] (n.) | 論壇，座談會

The social media forum will be held in Taipei.
社群媒體論壇將在臺北召開。

14. redesign [ridɪ`zaɪn] (v.) | 重新設計

The book's cover was redesigned for the new edition.
書本封面為了新版本而重新設計。

15. leave sb./sth. out | 除去；撇開；遺漏

Before we conclude the meeting, let's make sure we haven't left anything out.
會議結束之前，我們確認一下是否有遺漏任何東西。

Jenny didn't invite me to her party. Do you think she left me out on purpose?
珍妮沒有邀請我參加她的派對，你覺得她是故意把我屏除在外嗎？

16. feature [`fitʃə] (n.) | 特色，功能

There's a lot of new features on the new smartphone.
新款手機有許多新功能。

17. abbreviate [ə`brivɪˌet] (v.) | 縮寫成；簡稱

NBA star Lebron James' name is often abbreviated as LBJ.
NBA 球星勒布朗詹姆士的名字經常被縮寫為 LBJ。

18. figure [`fɪg(j)ə] (n.) | 數字

There's something fishy about the figures in this financial report.
財務報告裡的數字有些可疑。

19. **speculate** [ˈspɛkjəˌlet] *(v.)* | 猜測，推斷

People at the office are speculating that Tommy and Gina may get married this year.
辦公室都在猜湯米和吉娜可能今年結婚。

......

20. **obsess about/over** | 對……著迷、過分擔心
be obsessed by/with | 被……吸引而沉迷

兩種在用法上稍微不同，前者是主動形式「對……著迷，過分擔心」，
後者是被動形式「被……吸引而陷入沉迷」，但是意思基本上是一樣的。

My friend is always staring at the mirror and obsessing over his hair.
我朋友總是在照鏡子時自戀地看著自己的頭髮。

Tommy is totally obsessed with Gina. He just can't take his eyes off her.
湯米深深對吉娜著迷，他根本無法把視線從她身上移開。

......

21. **interaction** [ˌɪntəˈrækʃən] *(n.)* | 互動

Working in sales involves frequent interaction with customers.
做業務工作要經常跟客戶互動。

......

22. **go downhill** | 每況愈下

走下坡路，顧名思義就是「每況愈下」的意思。

The quality of the food at that restaurant has really gone downhill.
那家餐廳的食物品質真的越來越差。

Time is kind of an amazing thing because you can do so much with it. I think people underestimate time... I don't want to just sit on my phone for hours.

時間真的是一個很棒的東西，你可以拿它來做許多事。我想，人們低估了時間的價值……我不想整天只是在滑手機而已。

—— 歌手
Billie Eilish 怪奇比莉

Getting away from My °Digital Gadget

❶ digital gadget

數位裝置。digital 是「數位的」，如電子鐘稱作 **digital clock**，相反地，有指針的機械式時鐘就稱作 **analog clock**。gadget 是「小裝置，小器具」，小時候的卡通《G 型神探》就叫做 *Inspector Gadget*。

....

❷ digital wellbeing

數位健康。wellbeing 是指一個人的幸福和安康，如 **financial wellbeing**「財務健康」，**workplace wellbeing**「職場健康」，**emotional wellbeing**「情緒健康」，**digital wellbeing** 則是「數位健康」，說明人跟科技產品之間的關係。

A vacation getaway was just what I needed to take a break from my ¹**exhausting** daily routine work and recharge my batteries. So when Google called to ask if I'd like to take part in a three-day ²**summit** about ❷**digital wellbeing** in Thailand, I barely hesitated before ³**marking my calendar** and replying, "Yes." All I had to do ⁴**in return** was make a vlog about the trip and share the message.

The event ⁵**took place** at a luxurious South Pacific-style ⁶**resort** on the incredibly beautiful island of Koh Samui. I had a bungalow to myself that was big enough to ⁷**accommodate** four people, and even a private pool. In between ⁸**sessions**, we went on sunset cruises, enjoyed relaxing Thai massages and ⁹**savored** the delicious local cuisine. Talk about ¹⁰**living the life**! Merci, Google!

But don't ¹¹**get me wrong**. We—a group of social media influencers and ¹²**journalists** from around the world—weren't there just to ¹³**have the time of our lives**. In fact, all of the activities mentioned were part of a course to help us feel the ❸**JOMO (joy of missing out)**. In daily sessions, we learned about the science of digital wellbeing and how to better ¹⁴**balance** life and technology. We ¹⁵**evaluated** our tech habits and challenged ourselves to make rapid changes. I guess our group of influencers was there for a good reason—we're probably the most phone-addicted people on the planet. And if we can change, then so can everyone else.

I chose to try and ¹⁶**wean myself off** early morning phone checks—a longtime bad habit I've had that's a creativity and ¹⁷**productivity** killer. Thanks to the breathtaking scenery and ¹⁸**laid-back** ¹⁹**atmosphere**, I

丟下手機
跟著 Google 休假去

vith Google

025

#03

kind of enjoyed being ❹**offline** for the first couple of hours of the day. Now the only remaining challenge is if I can <u>sustain</u> this practice when I [20]**plunge back into** real life. [21]**Keeping my fingers crossed**!

In the end, I guess the key to digital wellbeing is not to [22]**get rid of** tech, but to coexist with it in a healthy and [23]**beneficial** way. [24]**Easier said than done**, but <u>definitely</u> worth the effort.

※ 底線單字為「複習單字」，為之前出現過的字。

❸ JOMO
(joy of missing out)

前一篇文章我們提到了 FOMO (fear of missing out)「社群媒體恐慌症」，JOMO 剛好就是相反的意思，即「享受與社群媒體隔絕」，意謂「因放下數位產品，不追逐社群媒體消息而帶來的喜悅」。

....

❹ offline

離線，為形容詞。相反地，「上線的」就說 online。「線上遊戲」就稱作 online game，不用網路也可以玩的遊戲就叫 offline game。

JR YouTube
影片 #5

經營 YouTube 頻道讓我養成許多不良的手機使用習慣。不過，最近發生了一件很有趣的事 —— 我跟著 Google 去到了美麗的泰國蘇梅島。在這三天的時間裡，我盡情丟棄了自己的手機，跟來自全世界的網紅們，一起研究如何促進數位健康。我不得不說，我很享受沒有手機的時光。

JR的話

Getting away from
My Digital Gadgets with Google

丟下手機
跟著 Google 休假去

在日復一日累人的例行工作之中，一場讓我逃離工作、休息充電的假期正是我所需要的。所以當谷歌打電話給我，問我想不想去泰國參加為期三天的數位健康高峰會時，我連猶豫都沒有，馬上拿出月曆記下，並回覆「我願意」。而我要做的就是用影片記錄這趟旅行，並將資訊分享出去。

這場活動在極為美麗的蘇梅島上、一座豪華無比的南太平洋風格度假村舉辦。我一個人就住在一棟足足可容納四人也沒問題的獨棟平房，裡頭甚至還有一座私人泳池。在研討會的空檔期間，我們出航去看日落，享受放鬆身心的泰式按摩，還大啖當地美食。這才是享受人生啊！感恩谷歌、讚嘆谷歌！

不過可別誤會了，我們這群來自世界各地的網紅跟記者，可不是為了享樂才來這裡的。事實上，上面提到的所有活動，都是幫助我們體驗何謂 JOMO（joy of missing out，享受與社群媒體隔絕）的一環。在三天的例行會議中，我們學習關於數位健康的科學理論，以及如何在生活與科技中取得平衡。我們評估自己的科技習慣，並挑戰自己迅速做出改變。我想，邀請網紅參與這個活動是再理由充分不過了 —— 我們大概是這世界上最手機成癮的一群人了。而如果我們能改變，那麼其他人一定也可以。

我選擇戒掉一起床就查看手機的習慣 —— 這是我一直以來的壞習慣，而這也是扼殺創意與生產力的殺手。多虧了這美不勝收的景色與放鬆的氣氛，我其實還蠻享受剛起床這幾個小時的離線生活。現在我唯一剩下的挑戰就是，回到我的日常生活之後，我是否還能持續這麼做。祝我自己好運！

最後，我想說，數位健康的關鍵並不是拋棄科技，而是以一個健康、平衡的方式與之共存。說起來容易做起來難，不過絕對值得你努力。

Vocabulary & Phrases
單字片語

026

※ 底線單字為「複習單字」，為之前出現過的字。

---

1. exhausting [ɪgˈzɔstɪŋ] *(adj.)* | **令人筋疲力竭的，令人疲憊不堪的**

The morning meeting was exhausting.
早上的會議讓我疲憊不堪。

---

2. summit [ˈsʌmɪt] *(n.)* | **高峰會，領袖會議，最高級會議**

---

3. mark one's calendar | **寫在行事曆上**

The summer summit will be held in Taipei on June 30th—please mark your calendars.
夏季高峰會 6 月 30 日在臺北舉行，請記得標記在行事曆上。

---

4. in return (for sth.) | **（以某事物作為）回報，交換**

| Jack: | Here, you can have these movie tickets. | 傑克：來，這些電影票給你。 |
| Tommy: | Wait, what's the catch? What do I have to do for you in return? | 湯米：等一下，你葫蘆裡賣什麼藥？我必須要做什麼回報你？ |

* What's the catch? | 當某件事好到難以置信，就用這句來問對方到底有什麼意圖、詭計或祕密，類似中文的「葫蘆裡賣什麼藥？」

---

5. take place | **舉行；發生**

| Gina: | It would be a real dream come true if our wedding could take place at a luxury resort in Hawaii. | 吉娜：如果我們的婚禮可以辦在夏威夷的豪華度假村的話，就真的是夢想實現了。 |
| Tommy: | You're dreaming if you think we could afford that. | 湯米：妳如果覺得我們付得起，那就真的是在做夢。 |

* luxury [ˈlʌkʃərɪ] *(n.)* | 奢侈，享受；奢侈品

6. resort [rɪˋzɔrt] (n.) │ 度假村；渡假勝地

---

7. accommodate [əˋkɑmə.det] (v.) │ 容納；為⋯⋯提供住宿或空間

The resort can accommodate two thousand guests.
該度假村可以容納兩千名房客。

---

8. session [ˋsɛʃən] (n.) │ （某活動的）一段時間；一場，一節

There will be three sessions in today's conference—one in the morning and two in the afternoon.
今天會議會共三個場次，早上一個，下午兩個。

---

9. savor [ˋsevə] (v.) │ 細細品嘗，享用（食物或經驗）

To be happy, it's important to live in the moment and savor each experience.
為了快樂，活在每個當下很重要，細細品味每個人生經驗。

---

10. live the life │ 活出精采、豐富的生活

是口語的慣用句，相關的片語還有 live the good life，形容「過有錢人的生活」。
live life to the full 則是「把人生活到最滿」，也就是「過著多采多姿的生活」。

Tommy went through a lot over the past few years, but now he's really living the life.
湯米前幾年經歷了很多辛苦，但是現在他真的活得很惬意。

---

11. get sb./sth. wrong │ 誤會、誤解某人；搞錯某事

Tommy: Gina, I'd have to rob a bank if we're gonna get married in Hawaii.

Gina: Honey, don't get me wrong. I love Hawaii, but I'm happy as long as I'm with you.

湯米：吉娜，我得去搶銀行才有辦法在夏威夷結婚。

吉娜：親愛的，不要誤會我了，我愛夏威夷，但是只要能跟你在一起我都開心。

12. journalist [ˋdʒɝnəlɪst] (n.) │ 新聞工作者，新聞記者

reporter 也是「記者」，那怎麼區分呢？reporter 一定就是 journalist，但身為 journalist 不見得就一定是 reporter，journalist 是廣義的新聞從業人員，記者、主播、編輯、攝影師等都包含在內。

The journalist stood her ground even when the interviewee lost his temper.
即便受採訪者中途發飆，該名記者還是堅守立場。

* lose one's temper │ 失去理智；發脾氣。意同 lose it。

13. have the time of one's life │ 享受快樂時光

跟 live the life 有點相似，但是更強調此刻、當下正在度過人生中最棒的時光，意思就是「極為享受，玩得非常開心」。

Gina: I heard you were really living the life during your vacation in Guam.	吉娜：我聽說妳在關島度假期間過得很精采。
Bob: Yeah, I had the time of my life! You should take some time off too.	鮑伯：對啊，我簡直玩瘋了！妳也應該找時間休息一下。

14. balance [ˋbæləns] (v.)/(n.) │ 取得平衡；平衡

Bob is balancing a book on his head.
鮑伯頭上頂著一本書。

15. evaluate [ɪˋvæljʊˌet] (v.) │ 評估，評價

Employee performance is evaluated once a year.
員工表現一年評估一次。

16. wean sb. off/from sth. │ 讓某人逐漸戒掉某事

wean 是「讓寶寶斷奶」的意思，可衍伸為「使某人逐漸戒掉或脫離某樣不好的事物」。

I'm trying to wean myself off sugar.
我試著戒糖。

The government is trying to wean people off dependency on unemployment benefits.
政府試著要讓人民戒掉對失業救濟金的依賴。

17. productivity [prədʌk`tɪvətɪ] (n.) │ 生產力

My supervisor said I need to step up my productivity.
我的主管說我要提升工作效率。

18. laid-back [`lebæk] (adj.) │ （口語）悠閒的，放鬆的

Jenny is so laid-back. She never seems to worry about anything.
珍妮整個人很放鬆的感覺，看起來總是無憂無慮的樣子。

19. atmosphere [`ætməs.fɪr] (n.) │ 大氣層；氣氛

The office atmosphere is great as long as the boss isn't around.
只要老闆不在，辦公室的氣氛都還滿好的。

20. plunge (back) in/into sth. │ 突然陷入某事

plunge 是「跳入；陷入；下跌」的意思，這組片語則是「突然開始積極地做某事」或是「突然陷入某事」，加上 back 則是強調「再度」開始做或陷入。

The man nearly died after his car plunged off the bridge.
那人的車子摔下橋，他差點死掉。

The stock market plunged by thirty percent due to the coronavirus outbreak.
股市因新型冠狀病毒爆發而暴跌百分之三十。

* outbreak [`aut.brɛk] (n.) │ （疾病或壞事）爆發，突然發生

21. keep one's fingers crossed / cross one's fingers │ 祝某人好運

將食指和中指兩根手指（fingers）交叉（cross），是代表好運，因此這麼說的時候，就是「祈求好運」。不過，小時候我們說謊也會在背後交叉手指，代表「我所說的不算數」。

Jack: If this doesn't work out, we might lose our jobs.
Tommy: Better keep our fingers crossed.

傑克：如果這行不通，我們可能會丟了飯碗。
湯米：那我們最好開始祈求好運。

22. get rid of ｜除掉，擺脫掉

It can be difficult for schools to get rid of bad teachers.
學校要開除不適任的老師並不容易。

How on earth are we gonna get rid of all this old furniture?
我們究竟要怎麼處理掉這些舊傢俱？

23. beneficial [ˌbɛnəˈfɪʃəl] (adj.) ｜有益的，有用的

The training course should be beneficial to our team's productivity.
訓練課程應該會對團隊的生產力有所幫助。

24. easier said than done ｜說的比做的簡單

這是口語說法，也就是「說的比做的容易」。
另一個類似說法則是 easy for you to say「你說得倒是輕鬆」。

Jack:	Maybe we should rewrite the entire plan.	傑克：也許我們應該重寫整個計畫。
Tommy:	That's easier said than done. We're on a tight schedule.	湯米：說得容易，我們時間很緊迫。
Jack:	I have an idea! Let's just tell the client we have a better proposal and we need more time to polish it.	傑克：我想到一個點子！我們就告訴客戶我們有一個更好的提案，需要多一點時間修飾它。
Tommy:	That's easy for you to say. I'm the one who's gonna have to tell them.	湯米：你說得倒是輕鬆，要跟他們說的人還不是我。

* a tight schedule ｜行程緊湊

More Expressions
Social Media 社群媒體用語

block (v.) | 封鎖

Do you think I should delete hate comments, or just block them?

你覺得我應該刪除黑特留言,還是乾脆封鎖他們?

trending (adj.) | 發燒的

竄紅的影片都會登上 YouTube 發燒,
英文就是 trending;它不只是 YouTube 用語喔!
一般的對話裡中也可以用 trending,
代表「很熱門」的意思。

What are the latest trending topics?
最近的熱門話題是什麼?

livestream (v.) | 直播

stream 是指在網路上播放影片或音源,live
就是「現場」,所以 live + stream 就是「直播」的意
思,直播主則叫做 livestreamer。
在其他平臺上也可以用這個單字。

He's a livestreamer who livestreams
seven days a week.
他是一位直播主,一個禮拜有七天在直播。

hashtag (n.) | 主題標籤

hashtag 就是大家常看到的「#」井字號,
用來描述主題或關鍵字。

like / dislike (v.) | 按喜歡 / 按不喜歡

在 YouTube 上除了按喜歡還可以按不喜歡,
在 Facebook 上則只有按讚 Like,Instagram
則是用愛心,通常也用 Like 表示。

LB / FB (v.) | 回按讚 / 追蹤自己

在 Instagram 上常看到,也就是 Like Back
和 Follow Back 的縮寫,
意思是自己幫對方按讚或追蹤對方了,
請對方也幫自己按讚和追蹤自己。

comment (v.) | 留言

pin (v.) | 置頂

原意是用別針別住,在 YouTube 和
Facebook 上則是置頂的意思。

OMG! My favorite YouTuber pinned
my comment!
我的天啊!我最喜歡的 YouTuber
把我的留言置頂了!

monetization (n.) │ 營利

在 YouTube 上開營利怎麼講呢？就是
enable monetization，更口語的說法，會用它的
動詞 monetize。

Let me tell you how to monetize your videos.
讓我來告訴你怎麼幫影片開營利。

easter egg │ 彩蛋

在影片中或者是結尾所放的隱藏畫面或訊息，
就叫做 easter egg。

social media manager
社群媒體經理，小編

TA〔target audience〕 │ 目標受眾

tag (v.) │ 標記人名

在 Facebook 和 Instagram 上標記人名
就是用 tag 這個單字。

Can you tag me in your photo?
你可以在照片裡標記我嗎？

caption (n.)／(v.) │ 說明文字，圖片說明

圖片下面的說明文字，也可以當作動詞使用。

What does Jenny's selfie caption read?
珍妮的自拍貼文寫什麼？

reach (n.) │ 觸及人數

What's the reach of your latest post?
你最新貼文的觸及人數是多少？

社群、網路流行用語

hater, troll (n.) │ 黑特，酸民

SJW〔social justice warrior〕
正義魔人

facepalm (v.)／(n.) │ 無言

想像把你的臉 (face) 埋在掌心 (palm) 裡，是不是
就是個無奈的姿勢呢？

LOL〔laughing out loud〕 │ 大笑

emoji (n.) │ 表情符號

meme (n.) │ 迷因；梗圖

meme 不僅指梗圖，也指影音類等任何在網路上瘋
傳的梗。最有名的梗圖之一就是黑人問號。

lurker (n.) │ 潛水者

只看文章、影片，但是幾乎不留言
或顯露自己意見的人。

stan (n.)／(v.) │ 狂粉；瘋狂迷戀

跟蹤者 (stalker) + fan (粉絲) = stan (狂粉)，
很好懂吧！也可以當作動詞使用。

epic fail | 大失敗

go viral | 竄紅

viral 指「病毒的」，用在網路世界意思就是「如病毒傳播一般迅速蔓延」，所以 go viral 就是竄紅的意思。

······························

Those facepalm memes are going viral on the Internet.

那些無言迷因在網路上紅爆了。

selfie (n.) | 自拍照

講「拍自拍照」會用 take a selfie。

screenshot (n.) | 螢幕截圖

「截圖」就會說 take a screenshot。

Silence is not always a sign of wisdom, but babbling is ever a mark of folly.

沉默未必是智慧的代表，但是胡說八道永遠與愚蠢畫上等號。

—— 美國開國元勳
Benjamin Franklin 班傑明富蘭克林

How a Photo of Jus
Fooled the World

❶ all-time / big-time

兩個都是用來形容後面所連接的人或事，all-time 是指「前所未有的（好或壞）」；big-time 則是「一流的；非常成功的」。後者也可以用 big time 呈現，當副詞使用，意思是「很大程度上；非常」，如 I messed up big time.（我徹底搞砸了。）

❷ cover

cover 作為動詞有許多意思，「覆蓋」、「掩護」、「包括」、「翻唱」等，在本文則是「採訪，報導（新聞）」之意，名詞則是 coverage。

❸ news anchor

新聞主播，也簡稱 anchor，或是 anchorman「男主播」、anchorwoman「女主播」。相似的字則有 announcer。anchor 一般指報導新聞的人，而 announcer 指的是「播報人員」，體育競賽常用 announcer。

A photo of Justin Bieber ¹**took the media by storm** in late 2018. It was a photo of the singer eating a burrito sideways while sitting on a park bench. This certainly ²**raised** quite **a few eyebrows**, since no one ³**in their right mind** would eat a burrito from the middle. And the media, along with the public, ⁴**relentlessly** ⁵**took shots at** Justin for acting like a ⁶**weirdo**.

A few days later, however, everyone was ⁷**caught off guard** when a YouTube channel called Yes Theory uploaded a video titled, "We Fooled the Internet w/ Fake Justin Bieber Burrito Photo." It ⁸**turns out** that the team hired a Justin Bieber look alike to stage the entire ⁹**scenario**, successfully ¹⁰**pulling off this❶all-time prank**. After posting the photo on several websites, it eventually went viral on Reddit. In less than 16 hours, the mainstream media ¹¹**caught wind** and started ❷**covering** the story. From ❸**news anchors** to talk show hosts, seemingly everybody was having a good laugh about the photo. Who would have thought that ¹²**the joke was** actually **on them**?

Was it to ❹**raise awareness** about ❺**fake news** or simply pull a ❶**big-time** prank? I have absolutely no idea why Yes Theory did it. Either way, this does ¹³**ring alarm bells** about how easily the Internet or media can be ¹⁴**manipulated**.

In my own experience, I've seen people ¹⁵**fall victim to** fake news before. I've seen how information was ¹⁶**fabricated** to promote certain people back when I was working in media. While it's unfair to ¹⁷**paint everybody** in the industry **with the same brush**, it's surely no secret that these things do happen. As media consumers, I think it's crucial

一張小賈斯汀的照片
騙了全世界

for us all to be ❻**critical thinkers**. Always be observing, learning and asking questions. Don't [18]**buy into** everything you see, read or hear. Always think twice 'cause there just might be [19]**more than meets the eye**.

※ 底線單字為「複習單字」，為之前出現過的字。

❹ **raise awareness**

提升意識，如 raise public awareness「提升公民意識」。

....

❺ **fake news**

假新聞。

....

❻ **critical thinker**

我們生活在假新聞充斥的世界，當然要成為一個 critical thinker「批判性思考的人」，不過 critical thinking「批判性思考」可不是到處批評的意思喔！而是指對所接收的訊息進行了解並加以判斷，而非全盤接受。可別誤會囉！

JR YouTube
影片 #6

JR 的話

這部 YouTube 影片出來的時候，我除了邊看邊笑了十分鐘之外，還心裡想著……現在真是一個大量接收資訊，卻無法等速消化的世代。如果說「了解是力量，無知是損害」，那麼最可怕的莫過於「自以為了解的無知」。

How a Photo of Justin Bieber
Fooled the World

一張小賈斯汀的照片
騙了全世界

中文翻譯

2018 年底，一張小賈斯汀的照片席捲了媒體，那是一張小賈坐在公園板凳上、橫著吃墨西哥捲餅的照片，這當然引起了不少人側目，因為任何一個神智清醒的人，都不會從捲餅的中間開始吃。媒體跟大眾則不停批評小賈的表現活像個怪胎。

不過幾天之後，一個叫 Yes Theory 的 YouTube 頻道，上傳了一部標題為〈我們用一張假的小賈斯汀吃墨西哥捲餅照耍了全網路〉的影片，大家才知道自己被耍了。原來，這個團隊雇用了某個長得超像小賈的人演出一場戲，成功策劃了這起空前的惡作劇。他們在數個網站上貼出這張照片，最終在 Reddit引爆討論，短短 16 個小時之內，主流媒體便捕捉到風聲並開始報導這起事件。從新聞主播到脫口秀主持人，每個人都笑得樂不可支。誰曉得，到頭來被當笑話的其實是他們自己。

無論是要引起大眾對假新聞的關注，又或者只是想搞個天大的惡作劇，我完全不曉得 Yes Theory 為什麼要這麼做。無論是哪個理由，這件事確實警醒我們：網路或媒體影響力是能輕易被操控的。

在我自己的經驗中，我曾看過人們成為假新聞的受害者。過去在媒體圈工作時，我曾看過資訊被捏造出來，只為了幫某些特定人士宣傳。當然，要說這產業的所有人都是如此，未免有失公正，但是這的確是個公開的祕密。身為媒體消費者，我覺得擁有批判性思維是很重要的。永遠要記得觀察、學習、提問。不要看見什麼、讀了什麼、聽到什麼就照單全收，總是要三思而後行，因為事情也許比你想像中來得不單純。

Vocabulary & Phrases
單字片語

028

※ 底線單字為「複習單字」，為之前出現過的字。

---

1. take sb./sth. by storm │ 大獲成功；完全征服

Jenny's performance took the <u>audience</u> by storm.
珍妮的表演贏得觀眾滿堂喝采。

---

2. raise (a few) eyebrows │ 引起側目

如果做了某事讓他人揚起眉毛（eyebrows），就表示「讓人感到驚訝、不可思議」。

Bob raised a few eyebrows when he started crying like a baby on the flight.
鮑伯在飛機上像嬰兒一樣嚎啕大哭起來，引起不少人側目。

---

3. in one's right mind │（口語）神智清醒的

用在口語上，常用否定句表達，如 No one in his right mind would...（精神正常的人才不會⋯⋯），
或者 He's not in his right mind.（他失去理智。）

(Bob puts a piece of cake in his mouth.)
Tommy: Are you in your right mind? Didn't you just pick that up off the floor?

（鮑伯將一塊蛋糕塞進嘴裡。）
湯米：你還好嗎！它不是你剛從地上撿起來的嗎？

---

4. relentlessly [rɪ`lɛntlɪslɪ] (adv.) │ 持續嚴厲地；持續強烈地

The media has relentlessly criticized the president for his attitude about the virus <u>outbreak</u>.
媒體砲火猛烈批評總統對疫情爆發的態度。

5. take a (pot) shot at sb./sth. | （未經思量）貿然批評某人或某事

| Jack: | Now before everybody starts taking pot shots at me, let me just explain... | 傑克：好的，在大家開始大肆批評我所做的決定之前，容許我解釋…… |
| Bob: | Explain what? Explain how sorry you are? | 鮑伯：解釋什麼？解釋你有多抱歉嗎？ |

....

6. weirdo [ˋwɪrdo] (n.) | 怪胎

weird 是形容詞，「怪異的」意思，weirdo 則是指「怪胎，怪人」。

Bob is such a weirdo.
鮑伯真是個怪胎。

....

7. catch sb. off guard | 使某人措手不及；趁某人不注意

這個片語在本文是以被動式呈現，變成 everyone was caught off guard，
指每個人都被這個影片耍了、來不及反應。

Tommy:	What did you say when Alan proposed to you?	湯米：艾倫跟你求婚的時候，妳怎麼說？
Jenny:	I didn't know what to say. He caught me completely off guard.	珍妮：我不知道該說什麼，我完全沒有準備好。
Tommy:	So I guess you didn't say yes, ha-ha.	湯米：所以，我猜意思就是妳沒有答應囉？哈哈。

* **propose** [prəˋpoz] (v.) | 求婚，名詞是 proposal。

....

8. turn out | 結果是（尤指出乎意料的結果）

It turns out that Jenny didn't accept Alan's proposal.
結果珍妮並沒有接受艾倫的求婚。

How did the negotiations turn out?
談判的結果怎麼樣？

* **negotiation** [nɪ͵goʃɪˋeʃən] (n.) | 談判，協商

....

9. scenario [sɪˋnɛrɪ͵o] (n.) | 事態，局面，設想；情節

This is the worst scenario that could happen in this virus outbreak.
在這場疫情爆發中，這是可能發生的最壞局面。

10. pull (off) a prank (on sb.) | 成功整到（某人）

pull sth. off 是「成功做到（困難或出乎意料的事）」的意思；prank 則是「整人，惡作劇」，
可以作為名詞或動詞，表現方式可用 pull a prank on sb. 或者是 prank sb.，
因此 pull off a prank 是強調「惡作劇成功，成功整到」。

Bob:	Hey, did you pull it off? I mean that prank you were gonna pull on Gina.
Tommy:	Yeah, I did. And she gave me hell for it.

鮑伯：嘿，你有成功嗎？我意思是，你有整到
吉娜嗎？

湯米：有啊，然後她就給我好看了。

....

11. get/catch wind (of sth.) | 聽說，得知（某事）

尤指祕密或不為人知的事。

I don't want my coworkers to get wind of the fact that I'm leaving the company.
我不想讓我的同事們聽到有關我要離開公司的事。

Jenny:	I caught wind that Tommy's been flirting with a girl he met at a bar last night.
Gina:	It's probably just a rumor. He wouldn't dare!

珍妮：我聽說昨晚湯米跟在酒吧認識的一個女
孩子在搞曖昧。

吉娜：八成是謠言啦，他才不敢！

* flirt with sb. | 和某人調情、眉來眼去

....

12. the joke is on sb. | （口語）玩笑開到自己頭上

指原本想要耍或嘲笑別人，結果自己反倒成為笑料。

The mainstream media was taking pot shots at the actor until they figured out they got it wrong. Now the joke's on them.
主流媒體不斷攻擊那位演員，直到他們發現自己搞錯了，現在他們反變成笑話了。

....

13. ring/sound alarm bells | 引起警覺

當警鐘（alarm bell）被敲響時，代表有緊急或危險的事，因此該片語用來形容「有發生壞事的預感」。

Even though Gina didn't believe the rumors, it still sounded alarm bells in her head.
即便吉娜不相信那些謠言，但她心裡還是敲響了警鐘。

14. manipulate [mə`nɪpjə‚let] (v.) | （常指以不正當手段）操控，操弄

其形容詞為 manipulative「操縱的」。

The anchorman was accused of using his media <u>clout</u> to manipulate public opinion.
該名主播被控訴利用自己的媒體影響力操弄公眾意見。

* **be accused of** ｜被控訴

....

15. fall victim to sb./sth. | 成為……的受害者，被……所害

The world economy has fallen victim to the coronavirus pandemic.
全球經濟淪為新冠肺炎流行病的受害者。

* **pandemic** [pæn`dɛmɪk] (n.)/(adj.) ｜流行病；大規模流行的

....

16. fabricate [`fæbrɪ‚ket] (v.) | 捏造，虛構；偽造

Jack fabricated the report to make the numbers look better to the client.
傑克偽造客戶報告，好讓數字看起來好看一點。

....

17. paint/tar sb./sth. with the same brush | （貶義）以偏概全，一竿子打翻一船人

Not everybody in the company is like Jack. Don't paint us with the same brush.
公司裡不是每個人都像傑克一樣，不要一竿子打翻一船人。

....

18. buy into sth. | 照單全收

常以否定句陳述。

I can't believe you bought into that article. It's totally fake news.
我不敢相信你對那文章信以為真，那根本就是假新聞。

....

19. more (to sb./sth.) than meets the eye | 不像表面那麼簡單

字面上的意思是「比起眼睛所見的還要多」，也就是「不像表面那麼簡單」的意思。

I wouldn't buy into what the media is saying about the scandal. There's more to this situation than meets the eye.
我是不會相信媒體講的關於那起醜聞的事，事情不像表面上那麼簡單。

* **scandal** [`skændəl] (n.) ｜醜聞

Money and fame made me believe I was entitled. I was wrong and foolish.

金錢和名譽曾一度讓我相信我是有特權的。我真是大錯特錯又愚蠢。

—— 高爾夫球名將
Tiger Woods 老虎伍茲

Do All Child Stars [1] Crash and Burn?

❶ star

明星。如 NBA star「NBA 球星」，rising star「崛起中的新星」，但是作動詞的時候是「主演，擔任主角」之意，而這裡的 star in 則是「主演（電影）」，star with/alongside sb. 是「跟某人一起主演」。

❷ celebrity

就是 famous person「名人」的意思，簡稱 celeb。類似的稱呼還有 big name「有名的人」，hotshot「自信有成功的人」，icon「偶像」，personage「大人物」。

❸ spotlight

聚光燈，常使用 in/under the spotlight 表示，形容人「備受矚目的，成為關注焦點的」；另一個相似的片語是 in/under the limelight，但是前者是中性的形容，可以是好的或不好的受矚目，後者通常是正面的形容。

If you asked me to name a few famous child stars [2]**off the top of my head**, I'd probably mention Macaulay Culkin, who ❶**starred** in *Home Alone*; Haley Joel Osment, who acted alongside Bruce Willis in *The Sixth Sense*; and Lindsay Lohan, who is best remembered for playing twins in *The Parent Trap*.

You might be wondering, "How are they doing now?" When I read a recent post by Justin Bieber, who of course has become a pop superstar, I had the exact same question—"How is he doing now?" In Bieber's lengthy post, he brought up his rise to fame and how it [3]**took a huge toll on** his life. And it seems that many of these young ❷**celebrities** didn't [4]**handle** the ❸**spotlight** very well.

Macaulay Culkin was one of the most [5]**adored** child actors in the 90s. As the cute kid in *Home Alone* and *Home Alone 2*, Culkin won the hearts of millions. He left ❹**show biz** in 1994, a move he recalls as one of the best decisions he's ever made. After making 15 movies in seven years, all he wanted was a normal life. In a recent interview, he [6]**opened up about** his [7]**abusive** relationship with his father. "He was a bad man. He was abusive. Physically and mentally. I can show you my scars," said Culkin.

In countless cases of child stars gone bad, parental [8]**issues** [9]**stand out** as a key factor. Children, whose minds are still developing, are [10]**vulnerable** to negative effects from as the [11]**temptations** of money, popularity, romantic relationships, etc. And so it lies [12]**in the hands of** parents, who are supposed to be more [13]**mature**, to [14]**keep their children on the right track**.

童星註定都要崩壞收場嗎？

However, to [15]**put things in perspective**, [13]**maturity** and wisdom don't necessarily grow with age. You could be ❺**in your forties** but still act like a kindergartener. Wisdom is something we all need to intentionally work on in order to achieve. We need to be mentally and spiritually fit to deal with the many things we encounter in life, even the good ones. To make an [16]**analogy**: give a Lamborghini to a skilled adult driver and he'll ride like the wind; give it to a 10-year-old kid and he'll crash and burn.

※ 底線單字為「複習單字」，為之前出現過的字。

❹ **show biz**

biz 是 business「事業」的簡寫，show biz 則是「娛樂事業，演藝事業」的意思。

.....

❺ **in one's forties**

四十幾歲，in one's twenties, thirties, fifties 等，就是二十幾、三十幾、五十幾歲，如果要說二十幾前半、後半段則可以說 in one's early twenties 和 in one's late twenties，其餘以此類推。要特別注意，沒有「十幾歲」這種說法喔！

JR YouTube
影片 #7

金錢、物質、名譽或愛情，是生命中的祝福，人倘若有足夠的智慧，就能成為它的主人；反之，就只是它的奴隸。

JR 的話

Do All Child Stars Crash and Burn?

童星註定都要
崩壞收場嗎？

中文翻譯

如果你要我說出心目中前幾位知名童星的話，我大概會說：主演《小鬼當家》的麥考立克金、跟布魯斯威利一同演出《靈異第六感》的哈利喬奧斯蒙，以及因為演出《天生一對》的雙胞胎而讓人印象深刻的琳賽蘿涵。

你或許會心想，「他們現在都在做些什麼？」當我看到最近一篇小賈斯汀的貼文——毫無疑問，他也成了流行音樂界的超級明星——我的腦海中也浮現一樣的問題：「他現在在做什麼？」在這長篇貼文中，他提到他如何崛起成名，以及成名這件事如何對他的人生造成了傷害。看起來，這些年紀輕輕的明星們，許多都沒有拿捏好螢光幕下的生活。

麥考立克金曾經是九〇年代最受喜愛的童星之一。這位出現在《小鬼當家》以及續集的可愛男孩，擄獲了百萬影迷的心。克金在 1994 年離開演藝圈，他事後回憶，表示這是他做過最棒的決定。在七年內製作了十五部電影之後，他一心只想回歸一般人的生活。在最近的一次訪問中，克金公開談論自己飽受父親虐待的事情，他說：「他是個壞人。他在身心上都虐待我。我可以給你看我身上的傷疤。」

在我們眼前發生的無數個童星走歪的案例中，父母親幾乎都是關鍵原因。處在身心正值發展時期的孩子，相當容易受到金錢、人氣、感情誘惑所產生的負面效果影響。而這有賴於應該是比孩子更成熟的父母，來確保孩子走在正軌上。

然而，要正確看待上述問題的話，成熟與智慧並不必然會隨著年齡成長。你可以是四十幾歲，但舉止仍像個幼稚園大班。智慧是我們得刻意努力才能累積的。我們需要在心理與精神上同步成長，才能應付我們在人生中所遇到的諸多課題，即使面對的是好事也一樣。舉個比喻來說：把一臺藍寶堅尼跑車給一個技術成熟的成年人開，就有如乘風飛翔；把它給一個十歲小孩開，就會出事。

Vocabulary & Phrases
單字片語

030

※ 底線單字為「複習單字」，為之前出現過的字。

---

1. crash and burn | （口語）慘敗，一敗塗地

Tim spent hours memorizing his speech, but he got stage fright and crashed and burned.
提姆花了好幾個小時記住演說，但卻因為怯場而慘敗。

---

2. off the top of one's head | 不經思索、立刻想到

If you have any ideas off the top of your head, feel free to share them.
如果你現在有想到什麼點子，儘管分享出來。

---

3. take a toll on sb./sth. | 造成傷亡或損失

toll 是「傷亡、損失」的意思，因此這個片語有「造成傷亡、損失」之意。

The coronavirus has taken a serious toll on the tourism industry.
冠狀病毒對觀光業造成嚴重損害。

---

4. handle [ˋhænd!] (v.) | 處理，應付，負責

The CDC was criticized for the way it handled the pandemic.
美國疾病管制署因處理流行病的方式而飽受批評。

---

5. adore [əˋdor] (v.) | 崇拜；愛慕，熱愛

Tommy: I adore you more than anything else in the world, Gina.

Gina: What's the catch? Did you do something wrong again?

湯米：我愛慕妳超過這世上任何東西，吉娜。
吉娜：你葫蘆裡在賣什麼藥？你是不是又做錯事了？

6. open up about sth. │ 敞開心胸說出某事

It took a long time for Tommy to open up to Gina about his breakup with his ex-girlfriend.
湯米花了很長的時間，才對吉娜敞開心胸提到他跟前女友分手的事。

....

7. abusive [ə`bjusɪv] *(adj.)* │ 惡行惡語的；虐待的；濫用的

I wouldn't say Jack is abusive, but he is kind of <u>manipulative</u> when it comes to work.
我不敢說傑克愛辱罵別人，不過一講到工作的事，他控制欲是強了點。

....

8. issue [`ɪʃu] *(n.)* │ 問題；議題

I think Jack may be having interpersonal relationship issues. He's always so grumpy.
我覺得傑克人際關係可能出了問題，他總是脾氣暴躁。

* **grumpy** [`ɡrʌmpi] *(adj.)* │ 脾氣差的，易生氣的；愛抱怨的

....

9. stand out │ 顯眼，突出

Among all the applicants, there's one in particular that really stands out.
所有的申請者當中，有一位特別顯眼。

....

10. vulnerable [`vʌlnərəbl] *(adj.)* │ 易受傷的，脆弱的；易受影響（或受攻擊）的

Tourists are vulnerable to theft because they're not familiar with the area.
觀光客很容易被偷東西，因為他們不熟悉該區域。

Martha has been feeling vulnerable since her divorce.
瑪莎離婚之後，便感到很脆弱。

....

11. temptation [tɛmp`teʃən] *(n.)* │ 引誘；誘惑

Jenny gave in to the temptation of buying a new designer bag.
珍妮無法抗拒誘惑，買了一個新的名牌包。

12. in the hands of sb. / in one's hands｜在掌握之中

字面上意思是在某人手中，也就是某事在掌握之中。out of one's hands 則是相反的意思，指「某人無法控制」。

Eighty percent of the company's stock is in the hands of five percent of the shareholders.
百分之八十的公司股票掌握在百分之五的股東手裡。

It's not my call. Things are out of my hands.
這不是我能決定的，事情不是我能控制的。

* call｜這裡的 call 不是打電話，而是「決定」的意思。慣用的說法有 it's my call（我有決定權），it's not my call（這不是我能決定的），make the call（做決定）等。

13. mature [mə`tʃur] (adj.)｜成熟的

名詞為 maturity。

Gina is pretty mature for her age.
以吉娜的年齡來說，她算是相當成熟。

14. keep sb./sth. on the right track｜確保某人某事在正軌上

確保某人某事在正確的軌道（track）上，意思就是「確保某人某事不出問題」。

It's really hard to keep your children on the right track since there are so many temptations these days.
要讓孩子走在正途上真的很難，這年頭有太多誘惑了。

15. put things in(to) perspective｜客觀來看

perspective 有「透視圖法」的意思，因此把事物放進透視圖來檢視，就是「客觀比較；客觀審視」之意。

To put things in perspective, total sales have gone down by two percent, but our market share has increased by ten percent. That means we're getting by in a shrinking market.
客觀來說，我們整體銷售數字下降了百分之二，但是我們的市佔率上升了百分之十，這意味著我們在一個整體來講正在縮小的市場中表現得還算過得去。

* get by｜勉強過活；過得去，還可以
* shrink [ʃrɪŋk] (v.)｜縮水，縮小

16. analogy [ə`næləgi] *(n.)* | 比擬，比喻

常用以下表達：make/draw an analogy with/to/between sth.。

The professor drew an analogy between the human eye and the way a video camera works.
教授將人類眼睛比喻成錄影機運作的方式。

I never made it to the school choir because the music teacher didn't like my voice. I was pretty sad. But he was probably right; I did have a voice a bit like a goat, but my dad told me to never give up and to keep going, and it's paid off.

我從未入選學校合唱團,因為音樂老師不喜歡我的聲音。我當時非常難過。但或許他是對的;我的聲音聽起來的確有點像山羊叫,但是我爸爸告訴我絕不要放棄,要繼續努力,而這一切都有了回報。

—— 歌手
Shakira 夏奇拉

Adam Sandler's Pr
Told Him He Couldr

❶ household name

家喻戶曉的人。**household** 是「家庭、一戶」的意思，**household chores** 指「家事」，常簡稱 **chores**。**household expenses**「家庭開銷」，**household good/product** 則是「生活用品」，如毛巾、洗衣精、碗盤等。

❷ comedy / comedy sketch show

喜劇。**comedy sketch show** 則是「幽默短劇」，**sketch** 是「草圖，草稿」，因此 **sketch comedy** 這類型短劇通常有許多即興表演的成分在裡面。

❸ hit

指非常受歡迎或成功的人或事。以前我在廣播當 DJ 的時候，常講到 **hit** 這個單字，如 **Ed Sheeran's number one hit!**（紅髮艾德的冠軍歌曲！），至於專輯的「精選輯」則會說 **greatest hits album**。

Adam Sandler's success in Hollywood has made him a **❶household** name. Over the years, he's been in [1]**dozens of** movies, mostly **❷comedies**, including **❸hits** like *The Wedding Singer*, *Big Daddy*, *Click* and *Grown Ups*. Despite his fame, however, opinion on Sandler's acting ability is sharply [2]**divided**. In fact, his college acting teacher told him he wasn't [3]**cut out for** the profession.

Back in the 1980s, Sandler majored in art at NYU. On one [4]**occasion**, his acting teacher took him out for a beer to give him some [5]**genuine** advice. "Think about something else," his teacher told him [6]**earnestly**. "Listen, you **❹got heart**, but you don't have it. Choose another path."

Luckily, Sandler didn't take his teacher's advice. After appearing in small TV roles and performing **❺stand-up**, he got his big break in 1991 when he joined the cast of **❷comedy sketch show** *Saturday Night Live*. With SNL as his **❻launch pad**, Sandler began [7]**landing** movie roles and gradually [8]**made a name for himself** in Hollywood.

At the [9]**peak** of his career, Sandler was out with some friends one day when he happened to [10]**run into** the teacher who told him he didn't [11]**have what it takes**. What an opportunity to [12]**rub it in his face** and take his sweet revenge! Instead, Sandler walked up to his teacher, introduced him to his friends and said, "This is the only teacher to ever buy me a beer."

He could have [13]**made a fool out of** his teacher in front of his friends. It would have made him look good. But instead, he [14]**took the high road** and even had the [15]**courtesy** to [16]**compliment** his teacher.

亞當山德勒的教授告訴他不會演戲

031

#06

This story reminds me that people who are truly humble and [17]**grateful** are the ones that have real [18]**class**. [19]**On the surface**, it may seem like success defines who we are, but it doesn't. [20]**On the contrary**, it's who we are that defines our success. And it's the little things we do in life that [21]**show our true colors**.

※ 底線單字為「複習單字」，為之前出現過的字。

④ got heart

形容一個人「很有心」。

....

⑤ stand-up

單口相聲，單人喜劇。

....

⑥ launch pad

或作 launching pad，指火箭發射臺，衍伸指幫助自己開始做某件事的人事物，類似中文的「跳板」。

JR YouTube
影片 #8

從小到大我都記得老媽總是掛在嘴邊的一句話：「整瓶水不響，半瓶水響叮噹。」長大後越來越能感受到這句話的蘊意，一個人的氣度會顯出一個人的高度。

JR的話

Adam Sandler's Professor
Told Him He Couldn't Act

亞當山德勒的教授
告訴他不會演戲

中文翻譯

亞當山德勒在好萊塢的成功，讓他成為家喻戶曉的名字。這數年來，他出現在數十部電影當中，其中多半都是喜劇，包括熱門強片，像是《婚禮歌手》、《冒牌老爸》、《命運好好玩》跟《亞當轉大人》。不過即使亞當山德勒這麼紅，有關他的演技倒是褒貶不一。事實上，他的大學演技指導老師曾經告訴他，他不適合演戲。

八〇年代，亞當在紐約大學主修藝術。在某個場合上，他的演技指導老師帶他去喝一杯，並且給了他誠心的建議。「考慮做別的事情吧。」他的老師認真地跟他說，「聽著，你很有心沒錯，不過你沒有演戲天分。選其他條路吧。」

幸運的是，亞當並沒有接受老師的忠告。他先是在電視劇裡演出一些小角色，並且從事單人喜劇表演，直到 1991 年他的事業有了重大突破，他加入了短篇喜劇節目《週六夜現場》。有了《週六夜現場》作為跳板，亞當開始接演電影角色，一步步在好萊塢闖出名聲。

在他的事業如日中天之際，有一天，亞當跟他幾個朋友出去，碰巧遇到了當時跟他說他不適合演戲的那位老師。這可真是大好機會，可以好好洗老師的臉，享受甜蜜的復仇！然而，亞當走向他的老師，將他介紹給自己的朋友，並說：「這是唯一一位曾經請我喝啤酒的老師。」

他大可以在朋友面前讓老師出醜，想必會讓自己看起來很得意。但是，他選擇高格調地回應，甚至是有禮貌地稱讚了他的老師。

這個故事提醒了我，那些發自內心謙虛並心存感激的人，才是真正有格調的人。表面上看起來，或許是成功定義了我們，不過並不是這樣。相反地，是我們的本質才定義了我們的成功。正是我們在日常生活中做的那些小事，才能顯示出我們的真實本色。

Vocabulary & Phrases
單字片語

※ 底線單字為「複習單字」，為之前出現過的字。

---

1. **dozen** [ˈdʌzən] *(n.)* │ **一打**

dozen 是「一打，十二個」的意思，half a dozen 是半打，如果單單使用複數 dozens of，
則是形容「很多的，數十的」意思。

There are dozens of flavors to choose from. What should I get?
有太多種口味了，我到底要吃哪一種？

---

2. **divided** [dəˈvaɪdɪd] *(adj.)* │ **分開的，分歧的**

動詞是 divide「分開；分歧」。

The teacher divided the class into four groups.
老師將班上分成四組。

They are deeply divided over the <u>issue</u>.
他們在這個議題上意見極為分歧。

---

3. **be cut out for sth.** │ **對某事有天賦；適合從事某工作**

Jenny is truly cut out for her job.
珍妮在她的工作上真的很有天賦。

---

4. **occasion** [əˈkeʒən] *(n.)* │ **特殊場合，特別時刻**

Jack only wears his suit on special occasions.
傑克只會在特殊場合穿西裝。

5. genuine [ˋdʒɛnjuɪn] *(adj.)* | 真的，非偽造的；真誠的

The signature on the check is genuine.
支票上的簽名是真的。

Gina is a very genuine person.
吉娜是個相當真誠的人。

....

6. earnestly [ˋɜnɪstli] *(adv.)* | 認真地；誠摯地

Jack and Tommy were earnestly discussing how to <u>handle</u> the new client.
傑克和湯米嚴肅地討論該如何應付那個新客戶。

....

7. land [lænd] *(v.)* | （口語）獲得，得到，贏得

Charlie's dad landed a job at the same company Jack and Tommy work at.
查理的爸爸在傑克和湯米上班的公司找到了新工作。

....

8. make a name for oneself | 揚名，成名

I know you wanna make a name for yourself, but take my word for it, you aren't cut out for <u>show biz</u>.
我知道你想在娛樂圈出名，但是聽我的，你沒有這方面的天賦。

* **take my word for it (= take it from me)** | （口語）聽我的，我說的不會錯

....

9. peak [pik] *(n.)* | 高峰；頂端

Th athlete retired at the peak of his career.
那名運動員在事業顛峰之際退休。

* **athlete** [ˋæθlit] *(n.)* | 運動員

....

10. run into sb./sth. | 偶然遇到（某人）；遭遇（困難），遇到（麻煩）

Bob:	I ran into Jack after work yesterday.	鮑伯：我昨天下班後遇到傑克。
Tommy:	What you're actually saying is you ran into trouble, right?	湯米：你其實是想說你遇到麻煩，對吧？
Bob:	You <u>read my mind</u>.	鮑伯：你會讀心術。

11. have/got what it takes (to do sth.) | 有足夠本事或能力（做某事）

Jack: Welcome aboard, Daniel. Do you think you have what it takes to cope with the stress of this business? We have really demanding clients.

Daniel: Well, I have a fourteen-year-old who just hit puberty.

Jack: Then you'll do just fine.

傑克：歡迎加入我們，丹尼爾，你覺得你招架得住這一行的壓力嗎？我們的客戶可是要求很多的。

丹尼爾：嗯，我有一個十四歲剛開始青春期的兒子。

傑克：那你準沒問題的。

* **demanding** [dɪ`mændɪŋ] *(adj.)* | 苛刻的，要求高的

* **puberty** [`pjubɚti] *(n.)* | 青春期

12. rub sth. in one's face | （口語）戳某人痛處

把某事拿來擦（rub）某人的臉（face），意思是故意在對方面前提起會讓對方感到尷尬或做錯的事。

Bob: Hey, Tommy! Jack thought I was aiming too high with the forecast, but it turns out it's consistent with the monthly sales numbers that just came out.

Tommy: Way to go, pal! Now you have something you can rub in his face.

鮑伯：嘿，湯米！傑克以為我的預測數字下太高，結果它跟剛出爐的月銷售數字是相符的。

湯米：太棒了，兄弟！現在你有東西可以拿來洗他臉了。

* **forecast** [`for.kæst] *(n.)/(v.)* | 預測，預報

* **be consistent with** | 與……一致

* **Way to go!** | （口語）（表示贊同、興奮或揶揄他人）很好！真棒！

13. make a fool (out) of sb. | （口語）讓某人出醜，愚弄某人

口語中也會聽到 make a fool of oneself，指「讓自己出醜」，也就是「讓自己出洋相」。

Jack made a fool of himself by doubting Bob's forecast.
傑克懷疑鮑伯的預測，結果讓自己出盡洋相。

14. take the high road │以高尚的方式回應他人，以德報怨

當別人錯誤地對待自己，但是自己選擇用有格調、正當、有人格的方式回應，這時就會說 I took the high road. 類似「以德報怨」。

Tommy:	You know, Bob. On second thought, I think you should take the high road with Jack.
Bob:	Yeah, maybe you're right.

湯米：你知道嗎，鮑伯，我再想想之後，我覺得你應該要原諒傑克。

鮑伯：是啊，也許你是對的。

15. courtesy [ˋkɝtəsɪ] (n.) │謙恭有禮的舉止，禮貌

Jack should have had the courtesy to at least apologize to Bob for getting him wrong.
傑克既然誤會鮑伯，至少應該要懂得對他說聲抱歉才對。

16. compliment [ˋkɑmpləmənt] (n.)/(v.) │讚美，恭維

Everybody needs a compliment sometimes.
每個人偶爾都需要被讚美一下。

17. grateful [ˋgretfəl] (adj.) │感激的，表示感謝的

I'm grateful for having the opportunity to work here. A month ago I was still fretting about how to pay the bills.
我對於能在這裡工作心存感謝，一個月前我還在煩惱著該怎麼繳清帳單。

* **fret about/over sth.** │為某事煩惱

* **pay the bills** │字面是付帳單的意思，衍伸為「支付日常所需一切費用」。

18. class [klæs] (n.) │格調；風度；優異；高品質

The candidate showed real class when he lost to his opponent in the election.
該候選人選舉輸給了對手後，展現了真正的風度。

* **candidate** [ˋkændɪˌdet] (n.) │候選人；求職應試者

* **opponent** [əˋponənt] (n.) │對手

19. on the surface ｜表面上

Everything looks fine on the surface, but deep down Jack and Bob really don't like each other.
傑克和鮑伯表面上都相安無事，但是他們其實並不喜歡彼此。

* **deep down** ｜在內心深處

....

20. on the contrary ｜相反地，恰恰相反

I thought the final episode would be good. On the contrary, it was totally boring.
我以為最後一集會很好看，恰恰相反，簡直無聊透了。

* **episode** [ˋɛpə͵sod] *(n.)* ｜（影集、電影、廣播節目的）一集

....

21. show one's true colors ｜露出真面目

I thought Rick was my friend, but he showed his true colors when I asked for help.
我以為瑞克是我的朋友，但是當我向他求助時，他就露出真面目了。

More Expressions
Mass Media 大眾媒體用語

latest news｜最新新聞

breaking news｜重大新聞

exclusive news｜獨家新聞

top story｜重點新聞，焦點新聞

in the news｜上新聞

(news) just in｜剛收到最新新聞

make (the) headlines｜上頭條新聞

Tommy: Hey, you're in the news!（You're all over the news!）
Gina: I know, I made the headlines.

湯米：嘿，妳上新聞了！（新聞都在報導妳耶！）
吉娜：我知道，我上頭條了。

back to sb.｜將鏡頭交回某人

Anchorman: We have breaking news just in. This is live from Australia, over to you Jennifer.
Reporter: Thank you, Roger. I'm reporting live from Sydney... Back to you, Roger.

主播：我們剛收到重大新聞消息，來自澳洲現場，我們交給珍妮佛。
記者：謝謝羅傑，我現在人在雪梨現場直播……交還給棚內主播羅傑。

live in/at/from｜在（某地）現場直播

coming up next｜接下來（播出、報導）

at the top of the hour/at the bottom of the hour｜本鐘頭前半/後半

top 是「頂端」，bottom 是「底端」，所以在一個小時的頂端或底端，分別就是一個小時的開端或是下半段。

Coming up next at the bottom of the hour is our exclusive interview with world-renowned author JR Lee.

接著在本鐘頭後半段是我們對世界知名作家 JR Lee 的獨家專訪。

tune in｜收聽；收看

don't touch that dial｜不要轉臺

dial 是舊式的「撥號錶盤」，不要碰那撥號錶盤的意思，就是「不要轉臺」。一般是節目主持人對聽眾或觀眾講的口語說法。也可以說 stay tuned，當然也可以更直白地說 Don't go away, we'll be right back.（不要走開，我們馬上回來。）

Thank you very much for tuning in to ICRT. We'll be right back after a short break, so don't touch that dial.

感謝收聽 ICRT，我們稍微休息片刻馬上回來，不要轉臺。

no news is good news 沒消息就是好消息	**behind closed doors** 關門地，不公開地
bad news travels fast ｜ 壞事傳千里	**raise/lift the curtain** 公開某事，揭露細節或真相

媒體事物名稱

tabloid (n.) / (adj.) ｜ **通俗小報；通俗小報的**

tabloid 原本指比一般報紙（newspaper）小一半的報紙，多半報導庶民有興趣的八卦新聞，現在延伸稱呼這一類報導風格的各種文字媒體。

scoop (n.) ｜ **（美式口語）獨家新聞，搶先報導的新聞；最新資訊或消息**

the press ｜ 報社；新聞界；記者們

press conference ｜ 記者會

pressroom (n.) ｜ 記者室

Boss: When is the press conference?
Employee: Right now, boss. The press is waiting for you in the conference room.

老闆：記者會是什麼時候？
職員：老闆，就是現在，記者們已經在記者室等你。

publicity (n.) ｜ 宣傳，推廣；大眾關注

hard news
硬性新聞，嚴肅重要的新聞

soft news
軟性新聞，輕鬆不重要的新聞

publicity (n.) ｜ 宣傳，推廣；大眾關注

Tommy: What's the scoop on Justin Bieber in the tabloids?
Gina: Nothing newsworthy, just some soft news on his Instagram posts.

湯米：八卦小報裡有什麼小賈斯汀的消息？
吉娜：沒什麼報導價值的，就一些關於他 Instagram 貼文的軟性新聞。

host (n.) / (v.) │ **主持人；主持（電視或廣播）**

sports broadcaster │ **體育播報員**

體育播報員可以進一步分為 play-by-play announcer「播報員」和 color commentator「球評」，前者負責播報競賽場上的實況，後者則以自身專業經驗補充評論，也經常用 sports announcer 或 sports commentator 表達。

cameraman (n.) │ **男攝影師**

camerawoman (n.) │ **女攝影師**

source (n.) │ **消息來源；提供消息來源者**

whistle-blower (n.)
吹哨者，揭密者，告密者

正能量
座右銘
MOTTO

I prefer to win titles with the team ahead of individual awards or scoring more goals than anyone else. I'm more worried about being a good person than being the best football player in the world. When all this is over, what are you left with? When I retire, I hope I am remembered for being a decent guy.

比起得到個人獎項或是比任何人進更多球，我更想跟全隊一起贏得冠軍。比起成為全世界最厲害的足球員，我更希望成為一個好人。當這一切結束，你還剩下什麼？當我退休，我希望人們印象中的我是個很好的人。

—— 世界足球先生
Lionel Messi 梅西

The Warriors Lost
and Handled It witl

❶ NBA Finals

是 NBA 一年一度的總決賽。final 當名詞有「決賽」的意思，要注意，NBA Finals 是專有名詞，因此 Finals 首字母要大寫。另外，finals 也有「期末考」的意思。至於 NBA「球季」是用 season 稱呼，球季又分為常規賽和季後賽，分別是 regular season 和 the playoffs。球季前後還分別有 preseason「季前賽」和 offseason「休賽期間」。

....

❷ sideline

sideline 當名詞有「邊線」的意思，作為動詞時則常以被動式「（因受傷或表現不好）坐冷板凳」表示，也可以 說 sit on the bench，如 The coach made me sit on the bench.（教練讓我坐冷板凳。）「板凳球員」則是 benchwarmer，顧名思義，是負責把板凳坐暖的人。

For two weeks each June, basketball fans [1]**live and breathe** the NBA Finals. Even though I'm not a [2]**fanatical** NBA fan—the kind who sits in front of the TV watching every single game—I was still caught off guard when I heard that the Toronto Raptors [3]**upset** the Golden State Warriors to claim their first ever [4]**championship** [5]**title**. After all, the Warriors had won three out of four NBA titles since 2015. It was easy to assume that it wouldn't be hard for them to pull it off once again. [6]**Dead wrong**!

It had already been a rough season for the Warriors due to multiple [7]**injuries**. But when Kevin Durant and Klay Thompson were both ❷**sidelined** by injuries in the last two games of the Finals, I thought to myself, "Man, things are really going downhill." On the other hand, the Raptors were [8]**on fire**. They had a 3-1 lead after Game 4, beating the Warriors by double digits in both Game 3 and 4. The Raptors also [9]**had the upper hand** in Game 5, playing in front of their hometown fans in Toronto. But just when the championship was [10]**within their grasp**, the Warriors managed to [11]**edge them out** with a 106-105 win. This led to Game 6, giving the Warriors one last chance to [12]**turn the tables**. And [13]**the rest is history**.

But what really got my attention was when the Warriors took out a full-page advertisement in the Toronto Star to congratulate the Raptors on their first NBA title. The ad showed a picture of Warriors guard Stephen Curry hugging Raptors guard Kyle Lowry after the game with the text reading, "The Golden State Warriors congratulate the Toronto Raptors on their historic [14]**achievement** and bringing the 2019 NBA championship to the City of Toronto." This act of good

e °NBA Finals, Class

勇士隊展現運動家精神
雖敗猶榮

❸**sportsmanship** instantly ¹⁵**reminded me of** Luo Jialun's article 'Sportsmanship', which we read in our school textbooks ¹⁶**back in the day**. I've always remembered how Luo wrote about Wendell Willkie congratulating his ❹**rival** Franklin Roosevelt after losing the 1940 U.S. presidential election. It made such a good story! And I guess one day, the 2019 NBA Finals just might become a great story to tell our grandchildren.

※ 底線單字為「複習單字」，為之前出現過的字。

❸ **sportsmanship**

運動家精神；運動員風範。形容人很有運動風度也可以說 **He's a good sport.** 反之則是 **He's not a good sport.** 或是 **He's a bad sport.**

....

❹ **rival**

競爭對手；敵手。體育競賽中的對手一般會用 **opponent**，這兩字的差別在於，**opponent** 單純指競賽對手，**rival** 則表示雙方長期以來旗鼓相當或存有敵意。

JR 的話

寫下這篇文章的時間是 2019 年 6 月，看到勇士隊最後輸了 NBA 決賽有點訝異，不過，之後所發生的事情更是令我印象深刻。暴龍隊在多倫多慶祝勝利大遊行的當天，勇士隊買了全版報紙廣告祝賀對手奪冠。比起輸贏，一個人、一個隊伍的格調更勝一切啊！

The Warriors Lost the NBA Finals, and Handled It with Class

**勇士隊展現運動家精神
雖敗猶榮**

中文翻譯

每年六月連續兩個禮拜，全世界籃球迷都盡情享受著 NBA 總決賽帶來的激情。即便我不是那種會坐在電視前觀看每場球賽的狂熱粉絲，但我還是被暴龍隊逆轉勝擊敗勇士隊，贏得隊史上第一個總冠軍頭銜的消息給嚇到了。畢竟，勇士隊自 2015 年以來，四次決賽中有三次拿下 NBA 總冠軍頭銜。要假設他們會再次拿下冠軍，是很自然的事。但結果大錯特錯！

對飽受傷兵困擾的勇士隊來說，這是難熬的球季，尤其是決賽最後兩場，凱文杜蘭特和克萊湯普森分別因阿基里斯腱和膝蓋受傷下場時，我心想：「慘了，大勢已去。」另一方面，暴龍隊則是火力全開。第四場比賽結束後，暴龍隊已經取得了三比一領先，第三、四場比賽都以雙位數以上的差距擊敗勇士，第五戰還是在多倫多自家主場家鄉粉絲面前比賽，絕對是佔盡優勢，但是，正當冠軍頭銜已經勝券在握，勇士隊卻以 106 比 105 險勝暴龍隊，使雙方迎來第六戰，給了勇士隊反敗為勝的最後機會。之後的故事，大家就很清楚了。

不過，吸引我注意的，是勇士隊買下了《多倫多星報》全版廣告，祝賀對手贏得第一座總冠軍。廣告上放了一張勇士隊後衛史蒂芬柯瑞在賽後擁抱暴龍隊後衛凱爾洛瑞的照片，並寫著：「金州勇士隊恭賀多倫多暴龍隊達成歷史性成就，並將 2019 NBA 總冠軍頭銜帶到了多倫多市。」這「好球品」的行為，立馬讓我想起以前在教科書上讀過的一課，那就是羅家倫的〈運動家的風度〉。我永遠記得，羅家倫寫到溫德爾威爾基是如何在 1940 年的美國總統大選落敗後，恭喜對手富蘭克林羅斯福。這真是一個很棒的故事！我想有一天，2019 年的 NBA 決賽也能成為留傳後世的好故事。

Vocabulary & Phrases
單字片語

※ 底線單字為「複習單字」，為之前出現過的字。

---

1. live and breathe sth. │ 狂迷某事

描述因為太喜歡做那件事情，而把大部分時間花在上面。

Jenny lives and breathes ballet. She's been practicing since she was four.
珍妮非常享受芭雷舞，她從四歲開始就練舞。

---

2. fanatical [fəˋnætɪkəl] *(adj.)* │ 著迷的，狂熱的

It's hard to imagine how fanatical Europeans are about soccer.
很難想像歐洲人對足球有多麼狂熱。

---

3. upset [ʌpˋsɛt] *(v.)* │ 擊敗；使難過，使不安

upset 是「使難過；使生氣」的意思。但是在競技競爭方面，則是指「擊敗比自己強的對手」。

Liverpool upset Barcelona in the 2019 UEFA Champions League Semi-finals in one of the greatest comebacks in history.
2019 年的歐洲冠軍聯賽上，利物浦在準決賽擊敗了巴賽隆納，成為有史以來最偉大的反敗為勝紀錄之一。

* **comeback** [ˋkʌm͵bæk] *(n.)* │（競賽中）反敗為勝

---

4. championship [ˋtʃæmpɪən͵ʃɪp] *(n.)* │ 冠軍頭銜或地位；錦標賽

champion 跟 championship 有什麼不同呢？champion 是指得到冠軍的人，而 championship 是指「冠軍（地位或頭銜）」，也可以指「錦標賽」，如 NBA finals 就是一種 championship。

The team won a stunning victory in the championship.
該隊伍在錦標賽中拿下漂亮的勝利。

5. title [ˈtaɪtl] (n.) │ （體育）冠軍頭銜；標題

title 當名詞原本指「標題」，用在體育賽事就是指「冠軍頭銜」。

The boxer has a good chance of winning the heavyweight title.
那名拳擊手很有機會能贏得重量級冠軍頭銜。

---

6. dead wrong │ （口語）錯得離譜，大錯特錯

You'd be dead wrong if you thought Bob was dumb.
如果你以為鮑伯很笨，那你可是大錯特錯。

---

7. injury [ˈɪndʒərɪ] (n.) │ 受傷，傷害

動詞是 injure。

JR suffered a shoulder injury during soccer practice.
JR 在練足球時傷到了肩膀。

---

8. on fire │ 著火的；火力全開的

也可以用來形容人「非常熱衷」、「非常性感、有吸引力」，或是某人某事「非常成功，做得非常好」。

Lebron James is on fire! He's unstoppable when he's in beast mode.
詹皇手感超火燙！當他開啟野獸模式時，根本沒有人擋得住他。

* **beast mode** │ 野獸模式。形容人表現出超水準的力量、技術或決心。

---

9. have/gain the upper hand │ 佔上風

Tai Tzu-ying had the upper hand throughout the entire match.
戴資穎整場比賽佔盡上風。

---

10. within one's grasp │ 掌握之中，到手

在某人的手掌心之中，意思就是「某事十之八九成了」。

The deal is within our grasp as long as we figure out how to get in touch with their department head.
合約幾乎是到手了，只要我們想辦法搞清楚怎麼跟他們的部門負責人取得聯繫。

* **get in touch (with sb.)** │ 聯絡；取得聯繫

11. edge sb./sth. out │ 險勝某人或某事

Our high school basketball team edged out their long-time <u>rival</u> in the final 76 to 75.
我們的高中籃球校隊在決賽以 76 比 75 險勝我們的宿敵。

....

12. turn the tables (on sb.) │ 扭轉局勢；反敗為勝

The game was lopsided in the first two quarters, but we turned the tables on them in the second half.
比賽前兩節一面倒，但是下半場我們反敗為勝。

* **lopsided** [lɑp`saɪdɪd] *(adj.)* │ 傾向一側的，不平衡的；（競賽）一面倒的

....

13. the rest is history │ 後來的事就不用贅述了

剩下的（the rest）就是歷史了，意思就是「剩下的部分大家都知道了」。

When Tommy met Gina, it was love at first sight. He asked her out a couple of times, and the rest is history.
湯米對吉娜一見鍾情。他約她出去幾次，接下來的故事大家都很清楚了。

....

14. achievement [ə`tʃivmənt] *(n.)* │ 達成，成就

動詞是 achieve。

My biggest achievement in life so far is probably writing this book.
我人生到目前為止最大的成就，可能就是寫這本書了。

....

15. remind sb. of sb./sth. │ 使某人想起某人某事

....

16. back in the day │ 以前，舊時光

Back in the day, I used to play baseball with my friends after school. Seeing kids play catch in the street now reminds me of those good old days.
以前我放學會跟朋友們打棒球，現在看見小朋友在街上傳接球，讓我想起那些美好時光。

* **good old days** │ 昔日美好時光

正能量
座右銘
MOTTO

Remember that a person's name is to that person the sweetest and most important sound in any language.

記住，姓名對任何人而言都是最悅耳的語音。

—— Dale Carnegie 戴爾卡內基

How Nike °Blew Th[1]
with Stephen Curr

There isn't much space for competition in the Nike-[1]**dominated** basketball shoes market; as of 2019, Nike's market share in the United States sits at a [2]**staggering** 96%. In the NBA, three out of every four players have [3]**endorsement** deals with Nike. However, two-time MVP and three-time NBA <u>champion</u> Stephen Curry isn't one of them.

To [4]**set the record straight**, Curry did in fact have a deal with Nike up until 2013, when he started to [5]**make his mark** in the [6]**league**. He'd just scored a career-high of 54 points against the Knicks at Madison Square Garden, and by the end of the <u>season</u>, he [4]**set the record** for most [3]**three-pointers** in a <u>regular</u> <u>season</u>. Most brands were interested in ❶**cutting a deal** with Curry, including Nike, who wanted to hang onto the rising ❹**point guard**.

For Curry, in many ways, there was no reason not to re-sign with Nike. His godfather works for Nike, and he'd been wearing Nikes since college. So what led to Curry's decision to sign with Under Armour—a much smaller brand?

Well, just about everything went wrong at the ❺**pitch meeting**. At one point, Kevin Durant's name showed up on one of the PowerPoint slides. Apparently, someone had [7]**repurposed** slides from a prior pitch and forgot to change the name. And one of the Nike representatives even mispronounced Curry's name as "Steph-on." Curry's father Dell, who was also at the meeting, lost interest at that point.

Eventually, Nike chose not to match Under Armour's [8]**offer** of 4 million dollars a year. [9]**In hindsight**, considering the billions of dollars

Curry brought in for Under Armour in the following years, this was a terrible decision.

[10]**To be fair**, it wasn't the first time a big brand has misjudged an <u>athlete</u>'s [11]**potential**, and it certainly won't be the last. In his early days, Michael Jordan wanted to sign with Adidas. The German sportswear brand didn't see his potential, however, and [12]**turned** him **down**. But mispronouncing someone's name and not having the <u>courtesy</u> to [13]**tailor-make** a slide show for a million-dollar business meeting is [14]**a whole different story**.

To <u>quote</u> one of the famous principles in Dale Carnegie's book, *How to Win Friends and Influence People*, "Remember that a person's name is to that person the sweetest and most important sound in any language." <u>Get it wrong</u>, and it just might sound the bitterest.

※ 底線單字為「複習單字」，為之前出現過的字。

❸ **point guard**

（籃球）控球後衛，通常是運球傳球能力優越，負責組織進攻的球員。其他位置則有 **shooting guard**「得分後衛」，**power forward**「大前鋒」，**small forward**「小前鋒」，**center**「中鋒」。

....

❹ **pitch meeting**

pitch 可以作為「推銷（產品或點子）」的意思，因此 **pitch meeting** 近似於「提案會議」。

JR YouTube
影片 #9

JR的話

能言善道、富有個人魅力，這些對於一個人的成功絕對有加分，但並非必要元素。臺風、話術或是外在，可以在短時間內學習或打造出來。然而，一個人的品德與個性，是需要經過長時間累積的。而我認為，後者才是成功的真正關鍵要素。當你真心待人，他人是可以充分感受到的。

How Nike Blew Their Deal with Stephen Curry?

Nike 是如何搞砸柯瑞的合約？

中文翻譯

基本上，在 Nike 主宰的籃球鞋市場裡，沒有什麼競爭的空間可言，2019 年，Nike 球鞋在美國的市佔率就高達 96％，而 NBA 裡頭，每四位球員就有三位是跟 Nike 簽代言合約。不過，拿下兩次 MVP 與三次 NBA 總冠軍的史蒂芬柯瑞並不是其中之一。

說得更正確點，事實上，一直到 2013 年，當柯瑞正開始在聯盟裡打響名號之際，他都還是 Nike 的簽約球員。他才在麥迪遜花園跟尼克隊的比賽中創下生涯記錄 54 分，賽季結束時，他還創下例行賽最多三分球的記錄。許多品牌都對柯瑞非常有興趣，包含 Nike，Nike 想要留住這位崛起中的控球後衛。

從各方面來看，柯瑞都沒有不跟 Nike 續約的理由。他的教父在 Nike 工作，而且他從大學就一直穿 Nike。所以，到底是什麼事情讓柯瑞決定跟 UA，一個比 Nike 小上太多的品牌簽約？

只能說，在提案會議上，能犯的錯幾乎都犯了。有一度，凱文杜蘭特的名字竟然出現在投影片的其中一頁。顯然有人把前一場會議的投影片改一改就拿來用，卻忘了換掉名字。而且 Nike 的代表甚至將柯瑞的名字念錯，念成史蒂「芳」。一同出席會議的柯瑞爸爸，聽到當下便對這個合作失去了興趣。

最後，Nike 放棄跟進 UA 所提出的每年四百萬美金的簽約金。事後看來，以柯瑞接下來幾年替 UA 賺進數十億美金的獲益來看，這是個糟糕的決定。

說句公道話，這並不是第一次有大品牌錯估一名運動員的潛力，而這也絕不會是最後一次。麥可喬登年輕時想跟 Adidas 簽約，不過，這個來自德國的運動品牌並沒有看出他的潛力，因而拒絕了他。不過呢，念錯名字、沒有展現為百萬生意的會議客製一份投影片的誠意，這又是另一回事了。

引用卡內基《卡內基溝通與人際關係》一書所提到的著名原則之一：「記住，姓名對任何人而言都是最悅耳的語音。」搞錯的話，可能就會變成最苦澀的聲音。

Vocabulary & Phrases
單字片語

036

※ 底線單字為「複習單字」，為之前出現過的字。

1. dominate [ˋdɑmə͵net] *(v.)* │ **支配，統治；控制**

在文章中則是加上連字號 -dominated，變成形容詞，指「由……所支配的」。

There was a time when Nokia dominated the cellphone market.
諾基亞曾經一度主宰整個手機市場。

2. staggering [ˋstægərɪŋ] *(adj.)* │ **驚人的，令人咋舌的**

3. endorsement [ɪnˋdɔrsmənt] *(n.)* │ **背書；名人代言**

The celebrity makes a staggering ten million dollars a year in endorsement deals alone.
那位名人光是代言商品，一年就賺進驚人的一千萬美金。

4. set the record straight │ **（口語）澄清事實**

set the record 跟 set the record straight 有什麼不同呢？前者的 record 是「（成績）紀錄」，而後者的 record 則是「（資訊、訊息）記錄」，前者是「創下紀錄」的意思，後者則是指為了更正訊息而把話說清楚，意思就是「陳述真相，澄清是非」，兩者很不一樣吧！

To set the record straight, it was Jack who made the call, not me.
我先把話說清楚喔，做決定的人是傑克，不是我。

5. make one's mark │ **出名；成功**

近似 make a name for oneself。

6. league [lig] (n.) │（體育）聯盟，聯合會，聯賽

He strived to make his mark in Major League Baseball, but was soon demoted to the minor leagues due to a knee injury.
他相當努力想在大聯盟闖出名聲，卻因膝蓋受傷而被下放到小聯盟。

* **strive** [straɪv] (v.) │ 努力，奮鬥
* **demote** [dɪ`mot] (v.) │ 降級，降職，相反詞就是 promote，所以要說從小聯盟升上大聯盟，就用 promote 這個字。

....

7. repurpose [rɪ`pɝpəs] (v.) │ 重新利用；改變……的用途

During the virus underlined{outbreak}, a cruise line pitched the idea of repurposing their cruise ships as mobile hospitals to help meet the urgent need for medical care.
病毒爆發期間，一間郵輪公司提議將自家郵輪改裝成行動醫院，以滿足緊急的醫療需求。

* **pitch** [pɪtʃ] (v.) │ 這裡的 pitch 就同於主題單字中 pitch meeting 的用法，指「推銷、說服（想法）」。

....

8. offer [`ɔfə] (n.) │ 提議，提案；報價

....

9. in hindsight │ 事後來看

In hindsight, I think we should have taken the offer.
回過頭來看，我覺得我們當初應該要接受那個提議的。

....

10. to be fair │ 說句公道話

Gina: To be fair, the supplier's offer was pretty reasonable.
Jenny: Well, I guess there's no use crying over spilt milk now. What other options do we have?

吉娜：說句公道話，供應商的報價其實很合理。
珍妮：我想，現在後悔也沒用了，我們還有哪些選項？

* **reasonable** [`rizənəbəl] (adj.) │ 合理的
* **cry over spilt milk** │ 為了打翻的牛奶哭泣，意思就是「後悔也無益」。

11. potential [pə`tɛnʃəl] (n.)/(adj.) | 潛力，可能性；潛在的

12. turn down | 拒絕

The singer had great potential, but unfortunately he was turned down by the major record labels.
那位歌手很有潛力，但不幸地，幾間最大的唱片公司都拒絕他。

* record label | 音樂廠牌，也就是唱片公司，major record label 就是指如 Universal 環球唱片或 Sony 索尼唱片這種大唱片公司。

13. tailor-made [`telʌˌmed] (adj.) | 量身打造的

Jenny showed up to work today in a tailor-made dress.
珍妮今天穿著一件量身打造的裙子來上班。

14. be a different story | 和所想的不同；不是同一回事

用來表示「跟自己預想的不一樣」，常會在 different story 前加上 whole、totally、completely 等字來強調「完全」不一樣。

Rents are cheap in Kaohsiung, but Taipei is a whole different story.
高雄的房租很便宜，但在臺北就完全不是這麼一回事。

正能量
座右銘
MOTTO

Do not judge, or you too will be judged. For in the same way you judge others, you will be judged, and with the measure you use, it will be measured to you.

你們不要論斷人，免得你們被論斷。因為你們怎樣論斷人，也必怎樣被論斷；你們用什麼量器量測他人，也必用什麼量器量測你們。

——《聖經》馬太福音 7:1-2

Why Cristiano Ron Doesn't Have a Sir

❶ tattoo

刺青。**get a tattoo** 是 動 詞 說法，更口語的說法是 **get inked**。

❷ leukemia

白血病，俗稱血癌。「癌症」通稱 **cancer**，**leukemia** 和 **lymphoma**「淋巴癌」均是 **blood cancer**「血癌」的一種。其他常見的癌症則有 **lung cancer**「肺癌」，**pancreatic cancer**「胰臟癌」，**liver cancer**「肺癌」，**breast cancer**「乳癌」，**colorectal/colon/rectal/ bowel cancer**「大腸直腸癌」等，寫到這……希望大家真的要好好保持身體健康啊！

❸ bone marrow

骨髓；捐骨髓會說 **donate bone marrow**。

❹ charity / charitable

charity 是「慈善團體或事業；施捨，善舉」，「捐獻給慈善事業」會說 **give/ donate to charity**。「做慈善」慣用的口語說法是 **do**

Messi or Ronaldo? This is the biggest question in modern day football, or soccer, as it's known in the U.S. and Canada. "Who is the best player in the world?" If I had to choose, I would definitely pick Messi. Lionel Messi's skill and mentality on the pitch are just ¹**phenomenal**. But that doesn't mean I dislike Ronaldo. In fact, the more I get to know about him, the more he ²**grows on me**.

Cristiano Ronaldo ³**is no stranger to** being called confident, and even ⁴**arrogant**. He is currently the second-highest-paid athlete in the world, and isn't shy about ⁵**showing off** his luxurious life on social media every now and then. Ronaldo even has his own museum with a bronze statue of himself and a ⁶**plaque** reading, "Best Player in The World." He once told a reporter after being ⁷**booed** by fans of the opposing team, "I think that because I am rich, handsome and a great player, people are ⁸**envious** of me. I don't have any other explanation." I guess nobody describes him better than himself!

However, ⁹**amid** all the ¹⁰**flamboyance** and ¹¹**glamour**, it's rather interesting to find that Ronaldo doesn't have a single tattoo, which is rare in the football world. And the reason behind this ¹²**reveals** a totally different side of the ¹³**masculine** footballer. Having tattoos can prevent people from donating blood due to the risk of ¹⁴**infection**, and Ronaldo is a regular blood donor. He started donating blood when one of his Portugal national team teammate's three-year-old son was ¹⁵**diagnosed** with ❷**leukemia** in 2011. He also donated ❸**bone marrow** to the sick child. "Donating bone marrow is something a lot of people think is a difficult thing to do, but it's nothing more than drawing blood and doesn't hurt. It doesn't cost anything. It's a simple

do
e ❶Tattoo?

為什麼 C 羅身上沒有任何刺青？

process and then you feel happy because you know you are helping another person." Ronaldo said.

There are many other examples of Ronaldo's ¹⁶**bigheartedness**. In 2015, he was named the "most ❹**charitable** <u>athlete</u> in the world." And in addition to his ❹**charity** work, his incredible ❺**work ethic** has kept ¹⁷**propelling** him higher each time he seems to have reached ¹⁸**the top of his game.** That just has to make you think twice before you ¹⁹**judge a book by its cover**.

※ 底線單字為「複習單字」，為之前出現過的字。

charity work。charitable 則是「慈善的；施捨慷慨的」。

....

❺ work ethic

敬業精神。ethic 指「倫理，道德」，但是 work ethic 卻不能直接意會為職業道德，它是用來表現「一個人的敬業態度」，通常會說 He has a very good work ethic.（他非常敬業。）像是本文的 C 羅，他是足球界公認的訓練狂，即便已經三十幾歲，但是在各方面的表現、身體能力甚至比年輕球員還要強，這時候就可以用 good work ethic 來形容他。

JR YouTube
影片 #10

> **JR的話**
>
> 梅西在球場上的技術、直覺、精神和態度讓人看了熱血沸騰。然而，C 羅的勤勞和自我要求，讓人不得不認定他的成就。在球場外，他還是個愛心十足又愛哭的大男孩。每個人都有優缺點，當我們選擇看人的優點時，每個人都有值得我們學習的一面。

Why Cristiano Ronaldo Doesn't Have a Single Tattoo?

為什麼 C 羅身上
沒有任何刺青？

中文翻譯

梅西還是羅納度？在現代足球裡（美國和加拿大稱之為 soccer），「究竟誰是全世界最厲害的足球員？」這可是最難回答的問題。如果要我選擇，我還是會毫不猶豫選擇梅西。梅西在球場上的技術與態度令人歎為觀止。不過，這可不代表我不喜歡 C 羅喔。事實上，越認識 C 羅，我就越欣賞他。

羅納度的自信，相信大家都不陌生，甚至可以說他有點自大。他目前是全球第二高薪運動員，而他三不五時在社群媒體上炫耀他的奢華生活。羅納度甚至還擁有自己的博物館，館外有一座他自己的銅雕像，還用匾額寫著「全世界最厲害球員」。有一次，在被對手粉絲發出噓聲之後，他向記者表示：「大概是因為我有錢、長得帥、球又踢得好，所以人們才嫉妒我。我找不到其他解釋。」看來，沒有人比他還會描繪自己。

不過，耐人尋味的是，在五光十色的浮誇光環圍繞之下，羅納度身上一個刺青都沒有，這在足球界裡根本就是鳳毛麟角。而其背後的理由，則展現這位陽剛味十足的足球員相當不一樣的一面。身上有刺青的人，由於有感染風險，所以有可能無法捐血，而羅納度有固定捐血的習慣。2011 年當 C 羅在葡萄牙國家隊踢球的時候，隊上一名球員的三歲兒子被診斷出有白血病，從此他開始捐血。他也捐骨髓給這位生病的孩子。「大部分人聽到捐骨髓就覺得很困難，不過這其實跟捐血差不多，而且不會痛，也不花錢。就只是個很簡單的程序，但你卻會感到快樂，因為你知道你正在幫助別人。」C 羅說。

羅納度的大愛展現在許許多多的事情上。2015 年，他被稱作是「全世界最慷慨的運動員」。除了他所做的慈善，他不可思議的敬業態度總是能讓他一再超越自己的顛峰。光是這樣，就不得不讓你在用外在評斷他人之前三思。

Vocabulary & Phrases
單字片語

038

※ 底線單字為「複習單字」，為之前出現過的字。

1. phenomenal [fə`nɑmə.nəl] *(adj.)* │ 非凡的，傑出的，驚人的

If you get to know Bob better, you'll find that his knowledge of astronomy is phenomenal.
如果你有機會更認識鮑伯，你會對他淵博的天文學知識感到吃驚。

2. grow on sb. │ 某人漸漸喜歡上……

在一個人心中滋長，也就是說某事物逐漸為某人所喜愛。

At first I hated that song, but now it's starting to grow on me.
一開始我超討厭那首歌，但是現在越聽越好聽。

3. be no stranger to sth. │ 對某事毫不陌生

4. arrogant [`ærəgənt] *(adj.)* │ 傲慢的，狂妄自大的

With his arrogant attitude, he is no stranger to controversy.
他自大的個性讓他跟爭議總是脫離不了關係。

* controversy [`kɑntrə.vɜsi] *(n.)* │ 爭議

5. show off │ 炫耀，賣弄

show-off 則是「愛炫耀的人」。

Jack is always showing off his Lamborghini. What a show-off!
傑克總是在炫耀他的藍寶堅尼跑車，真是愛現！

6. plaque [plæk] *(n.)* | 牌匾

---

7. boo [bu] *(v.)* | 發出噓聲，喝倒采

boo 可以是指倒喝采的動作，也可以是喝倒采的狀聲詞。

(Tommy and Bob are at an NBA game.)	（湯米跟鮑伯正在看 NBA 比賽。）
Bob: You guys suck! Boooooo!	**鮑伯：**你們爛透了！噓！！
Tommy: Dude, stop booing the other team so loudly. People are staring at us!	**湯米：**老兄，不要再這麼大聲喝倒采了，大家都在看我們啦！

---

8. envious (of sb.) [ˈɛnvɪəs] *(adj.)* | 羨慕（某人）的；忌妒（某人）的

Jenny: I'm so envious of you and Tommy. You two are so perfect for each other.	**珍妮：**我好羨慕妳跟湯米，你們倆真的是絕配。
Gina: You'll find somebody that's worthy of you. Trust me!	**吉娜：**妳會找到值得妳的對象，相信我！

---

9. amid [əˈmɪd] *(prep.)* | 在⋯⋯中間，在⋯⋯當中；為⋯⋯環繞

Amid all the bad news about the <u>pandemic</u>, it was nice to see a story that gave people a sense of hope.
在充斥疫情的負面新聞當中，能看到一則帶給人希望的故事實在很棒。

---

10. flamboyance [flæmˈbɔɪəns] *(n.)* | 華麗；浮誇

---

11. glamour [ˈglæmə] *(n.)* | 魅力，誘惑力；迷人的美

The young designer was attracted by the flamboyance and glamour of the New York fashion world.
那位年輕設計師被紐約時尚圈的浮華和光環給深深吸引。

---

12. reveal [rɪˈvil] *(v.)* | 展現，顯露；揭露

Students are on pins and needles waiting for their test results to be revealed.
學生等待測驗成績出來的心情，真是如坐針氈。

* on pins and needles | 如坐針氈，坐立不安

13. masculine [ˈmæskjəlɪn] (adj.) | 男子氣概的；陽剛的

As masculine as he is, he cried like a baby when his dog died.
儘管再怎麼陽剛的一個人，當他的狗過世時，還是哭得像個孩子。

14. infection [ɪnˈfɛkʃən] (n.) | 感染

「（由細菌或病毒造成的）感染」之意，其動詞為 infect。

The viral infection can be easily prevented by just washing your hands regularly.
這種病毒的感染很容易預防，只要你經常洗手就可以了。

15. diagnose [ˈdaɪəɡˌnoz] (v.) | 診斷

Avril Lavigne was diagnosed with Lyme disease, which nearly took her life.
歌手艾薇兒曾被診斷罹患萊姆病，差點要了她的命。

16. bigheartedness [ˈbɪɡˌhartɪdnəs] (n.) | 善良，慷慨

bighearted 為其形容詞，如 a bighearted person（心胸寬大的人）。

17. propel [prəˈpɛl] (v.) | 推進，推動；激勵，驅策

propeller 是螺旋槳，而動詞 propel 則是「推進，推動」，可以是形容實際推動某物品，
或是推動某人去做某事。

The singer's bigheartedness propelled tens of thousands of people to donate to the earthquake relief fund.
該歌手的慷慨舉動，促使上萬人響應捐款給該地作為震災救濟基金。

* relief fund | 救濟金，救助金

18. be at the top of one's game/be on top of one's game

（做某事，尤指運動競技）在某人的鼎盛時期，巔峰狀態。

Even if I were at the top of my game, I'd still be no match for Lionel Messi. Which of course is a no-brainer.
即使我處在巔峰狀態，依然不會是梅西的對手。當然，這連想都不用想。

* be no match for sb./sth. | 不是某人某事的對手
* no-brainer | 毫無疑問的事，不用用大腦想就知道的事

19. Don't judge a book by its cover. | 不要以貌取人。

不要看到封面就判斷書的內容，意思就是「不要以貌取人；不要看外表判斷」。

Don't ever judge a book by its cover. There's always <u>more to people than meets the eye</u>.
絕不要以貌取人，總有令你意想不到的一面。

Whether you do or don't do something is determined by your 'thoughts'. However, it is a very small difference.

做與不做會左右於「想法」。不過，這兩者之間的差異其實非常微小。

——出自 JR 的筆記本

In Memory of Kobe
The Fall and Rise

❶ The Black Mamba

大家印象最深刻的，大概就是 Kobe Bryant 退休時講的最後一句話："Mamba out."「曼巴告退。」不過，黑曼巴這個綽號是怎麼來的？Kobe 本人在紀錄片 Muse 提到，他是從電影《追殺比爾》中用黑曼巴蛇殺死對手的刺客身上得到靈感。2003 到 04 年是 Kobe 人生的最低潮，他因一場最終以和解收場的性侵官司而身敗名裂，家庭也破碎，於是他創造「黑曼巴」這個分身，讓自己在心態上抽離這個窘境。場外的個人家庭問題，由 Kobe Bryant 來面對，在球場上就由黑曼巴來大開殺戒。Kobe 認為自己就像是條快速又致命的黑曼巴蛇。

....

❷ court

（籃球、網球、排球等）球場，也有「法庭」的意思。不同球類運動的球場稱呼不太一樣，「足球場」是 football/soccer field 或 pitch，「棒球場」baseball field 或 diamond。stadium 指「體育場」，如紐約洋基隊的主場就叫 Yankee Stadium。「高爾夫球場」golf course，「冰上曲棍球

On the morning of January 27, 2020, I woke up to the shocking news of the death of ¹**legendary** NBA star Kobe Bryant. ²**For a second**, I thought it was fake news. After all, people with nothing better to do these days are always creating celebrity death ³**hoaxes**. But as more and more reports came out, I began to realize that this was the real thing. Kobe was gone.

⁴**It goes without saying** that Kobe achieved numerous ⁵**milestones** in his career. But what makes him unique among all the great players is his "Mamba mentality." One ⁶**specific** game that displays it best would probably be the one played against the Orlando Magic on March 15, 2004. It was a time when Kobe was ⁷**in the midst of** a ⁸**controversial** ⁹**lawsuit** that wouldn't be settled until a year later. His life was ¹⁰**falling apart**. He ¹¹**winded up** getting kicked out of his own house. On game night, Kobe started for the Lakers, but his mind was somewhere else. He admitted it was the first time he didn't want to be on the ❷**court**. In the first two ❸**quarters**, Kobe played 17 minutes and scored… one point. His friend and rival Tracy McGrady, on the other hand, was ¹²**crushing it** with 21 points. By ❸**halftime**, the Lakers were ¹³**trailing** 50-61.

Kobe sat in the locker room during halftime thinking to himself, "You know what, you may lose everything in life because of the situation that you put yourself in. You may lose your family, your freedom, but I'll be damned if I lose basketball. Because this shit I can control."

In the second half, Kobe was a totally different person. By the end of the fourth quarter, the game was ¹⁴**tied** at 102-102. In ❸**overtime**,

Bryant: the Black Mamba

緬懷柯比：黑曼巴的失落與崛起

the Lakers <u>edged out</u> the Magic 113-110. Kobe scored 24 points in the fourth quarter alone, and ended up [15]**dropping 38 points** that game!

This specific game reminds me of how powerful the mind can be. All it takes is a little attitude [16]**adjustment** to change our actions, and even our lives. Sometimes what matters most isn't what's going on on the outside, but rather on the inside.

※ 底線單字為「複習單字」，為之前出現過的字。

場」 ice rink。拳擊雖然不是球類，但是「拳擊擂臺」稱 boxing ring。

....

❸ quarter / halftime / overtime

來看看籃球場上的各種時間吧，quarter 是「一節」，NBA 一節 12 分鐘，共四節，第一到四節分別是 the $1^{st}/2^{nd}/3^{rd}/4^{th}$ quarter，前兩節 first half「上半場」，後兩節 second half「下半場」，播報時常省略 quarter， 如 two minutes into the 3rd（第三節開打兩分鐘）。halftime「中場休息時間」，halftime break「中場休息」，overtime「加時賽」，NBA 是 5 分鐘，次數沒有上限。

JR YouTube
影片 #11

JR 的話

俗話說：「哀莫大於心死。」相反地，如果內心活著，沒有比這更大的確幸！即使你正經歷辛苦、感到灰心、自暴自棄、一蹶不振，但只要內心活過來，你的行為就會跟著復甦，生活也會醒過來，連同命運都會跟著翻轉。

In Memory of Kobe Bryant:
The Fall and Rise of the Black Mamba

緬懷柯比：
黑曼巴的失落與崛起

中文翻譯

2020 年 1 月 27 日早上，我一起床就被 NBA 傳奇球星柯比布萊恩逝世的消息嚇到。一時之間我還以為這是假新聞。畢竟，這年頭有人沒事就喜歡捏造名人過世的假消息。不過，隨著越來越多的新聞報導出現，我認知到，這次是真的。柯比真的離開了。

毋庸置疑，柯比在自己的籃球生涯中達成了無數里程碑，然而，真正讓他不同於其他偉大球星的關鍵，是在於他的「曼巴精神」。一場最能體現這個精神的賽事，大概就是 2004 年 3 月 15 日跟奧蘭多魔術隊的比賽。當時柯比身陷一場具爭議的訴訟之中，直到一年後才庭外和解。他當時的生活分崩離析，他被趕出家門。比賽當晚，柯比擔任湖人隊先發，不過他的心卻完全不在球場上。他承認，那是他第一次完全無心於比賽。前兩節比賽，柯比打了 17 分鐘，只拿到……一分。另一方面，他的朋友兼對手麥格瑞迪則是狂飆 21 分。上半場結束，湖人隊以 50 分比 61 分落後。

中場休息時間，柯比坐在休息室裡，他捫心自問：「你知道嗎，你有可能會因為自己的行為而失去一切。你有可能會失去家人、失去自由。但如果連籃球都失去，我一定會後悔。因為這件事是我可以掌控的。」

下半場，柯比完全變了個人。在第四節結束時，比分僅持在 102 比 102。加時賽，湖人隊以 113 比 110 分險勝魔術隊。柯比光是在第四節就拿下 24 分，整場比賽豪取 38 分！

這場比賽讓我反思，一個人的心智力量竟然可以如此強大。你只需要稍微調整心態，就能改變自己的行為，甚至改變自己的人生。有時候，真正重要的不是發生在外在的事，而是發生在內心裡的事。

Vocabulary & Phrases
單字片語

※ 底線單字為「複習單字」，為之前出現過的字。

1. legendary [ˈlɛdʒən‚dɛri] *(adj.)* ｜ **傳說的；傳奇的；著名的**

Lionel Messi is a legendary soccer player.
梅西是傳奇足球員。

2. for a second ｜ **瞬間**

在一秒之間，意思就是「頃刻間」。

3. hoax [hoks] *(n.)* ｜ **惡作劇，騙局**

For a second, I actually bought into that hoax.
有一瞬間，我還真的信了那個惡作劇。

4. it goes without saying ｜ **不言而喻，不用說也知道**

It goes without saying that Tai Tzu-ying is the best women's singles badminton player in the world.
不用說也知道，戴資穎絕對是全世界最厲害的羽球女單選手。

* **singles** [ˈsɪŋgls] *(n.)* ｜ （尤指網球、羽球、桌球）單打比賽，注意這裡的 singles 有 s 字尾。

5. milestone [ˈmaɪl‚ston] *(n.)* ｜ **里程碑**

Writing a book and having it published is definitely a milestone in my life.
寫書並且讓它出版，絕對是我人生中的一個里程碑。

6. specific [spə`sɪfɪk] *(adj.)* | 特定的，特有的

Gina:	On your way back, could you get me some pads?
Tommy:	Sure. Any specific brand?

吉娜：你回來的時候，方便幫我買衛生棉嗎？
湯米：可以啊，有特定的品牌嗎？

....

7. in the midst of sth. | 正當……的時候；在……之中

....

8. controversial [ˌkɑntrə`vɝʃəl] *(adj.)* | 有爭議性的；引起爭議的

....

9. lawsuit [`lɔˌsut] *(n.)* | 訴訟，官司

In the midst of the controversial lawsuit, the two parties decided to settle out of <u>court</u>.
在這場爭議的官司中，兩方最終決定庭外和解。

....

10. fall apart | 破碎；分崩離析

可以形容某個物品或群體，也可以是描述一個人的內心。

Bob:	Man, I'm falling apart. I'm barely breathing.
Tommy:	Dude, you OK? Wait... aren't those lyrics from Lifehouse's 'Broken'?

鮑伯：老兄，我徹底崩潰了，我幾乎無法呼吸。
湯米：老兄，你還好吧？等等……那不是 Lifehouse 樂團〈Broken〉的歌詞嗎？

....

11. wind up | 落得……下場，結果……

Your life is really falling apart. How did you wind up like this?
你的人生真的徹底在瓦解，你到底是怎麼淪落到這步田地的？

....

12. crush it | （口語）做得很棒

crush 是「壓扁、壓碎的」，也有「擊敗，徹底擊垮」的意思；而 crush it 是一個俚語式的口語說法，當某人做事做得異常地好、超越目標、勢如破竹，就可以說 You're crushing it!，是非常正面的稱讚。

Jack:	You're crushing it, Daniel! Keep up the good work.
Daniel:	Why, thanks.

傑克：做得不錯喔，丹尼爾！繼續加油。
丹尼爾：哦，謝啦。

* 這裡的 why 是感歎詞，可以表示驚訝、贊成、猶豫、生氣等。

13. trail [trel] (v.) | 落後

那在競賽中「領先」怎麼說呢？「領先」是 lead 或 in the lead，
如 leading by 24 points（領先 24 分）。

Liverpool is trailing Barcelona by two goals.
利物浦落後巴賽隆納兩球。

14. tie [taɪ] (v.)/(n.) | （競賽中）平手

He scored the equalizer, and now it's tied at 2-2.
他射進了扳平分，現在比數是 2-2 平手。

We were down the whole first half, but now it's a tie!
我們前半場本來落後，但是現在追成平手了！

15. drop point(s) | 得分

「得分」一般會用 score，而 drop point(s) 是專屬於籃球的口語說法，類似中文的「砍下⋯⋯分」。
不過在其他地方，這個片語其實是在說「下跌⋯⋯點」，這裡的用法差異要留意一下。

Stephen Curry dropped 21 points in the first two quarters.
史蒂芬柯瑞前兩節就砍下 21 分。

The Dow dropped 1,000 points.
道瓊指數跌了一千點。

16. adjustment [əˋdʒʌstmənt] (n.) | 調整；調節；微幅修改

動詞是 adjust。

After a few small adjustments to my bike, I was ready to hit the road.
稍微調整了一下我的腳踏車之後，我就準備好上路了。

* hit the road | 上路，出發

More Expressions
Sports 運動相關片語

通用

take sides｜選邊站

選擇支持哪一方，也就是「選邊站」的意思。

blow the competition away｜（美式口語）徹底擊敗競爭對手；輕易獲勝

no sweat｜毫不費力

不用流汗（sweat）就可以做到，表示「沒問題；毫不費力」。

棒球

out of one's league｜配不上某人

職業棒球有許多不同等級的聯賽、聯盟（league），在聯盟中要彼此競爭來進行排名。因此，形容一個人不到某事或某人的等級或水準，就會說 sth./sb. is out of one's league，在男女關係中特別有「配不上某人」的意思。

drop the ball｜失誤

棒球守備時球掉了就很尷尬，因此衍伸為「失誤，犯錯」，尤其指愚蠢或粗心的失誤。

take a rain check (on sth.)｜下次吧

早期棒球賽因雨延期時，會給觀眾一張未來可以使用的票，這個票就叫做 rain check，因此 take a rain check (on sth.) 衍伸有「下次吧，之後有機會再做某事」的意思。

網球

in full swing｜如火如荼地（進行當中）

網球揮拍（swing）沒有想像中容易，很容易把球打飛出去，因此當你可以盡全力揮拍（full swing）又把球控在場內時，表示「已經進入狀況」了。in full swing 就是指「某事進行到最活躍狀態」，get into full swing 就是指「某事進入最活躍狀態」。

the ball is in your court｜主導權在你手上

court 是指「網球、排球等球場」，字面上的意思是「球在你的半場；換你發球」，衍伸的意思則為「主導權在你手中；換你採取行動」。

高爾夫球

up to par｜達到標準，符合期待

not up to par｜未達標，不符預期

par「標準桿」是高爾夫球進洞的規定桿數，低於標準桿稱作 under par，因此 up to par 就有「達到標準」的意思。相反地，不到標準桿就是 not up to par，延伸有「未達標；不到一般或期望的水準」。

make the cut｜達標，晉級

源自高爾夫球，當球員達到或超越某個分數而免於被淘汰，就稱作 make the cut，衍伸為「因為成功或達到某項標準而被選上」的意思。

田徑

front-runner (n.) │ 最可能獲勝者；領先者

runner-up (n.) │ 競賽第二名，亞軍

也可以使用在各種不同的領域。

jump the gun │ 過早行動，言之過早

源自於田徑，在鳴槍聲還沒響之前就先偷跑，延伸形容「未經仔細思考就先行動」。

帆船

take the wind out of one's sails
挫某人銳氣，挑戰某人的囂張氣焰

航行時如果把船帆的風抽走，那船就會失去動力，很好理解吧，就是「挫某人銳氣」的意思。

go overboard │ 輕率行動

overboard 是「從船上落海」的意思，go overboard 衍伸有「沒有考慮後果，就輕率採取行動」。

拳擊

throw in the towel │ 認輸，放棄

拳擊比賽時，如果拳擊手將毛巾丟進場內就代表投降，所以就是「認輸，放棄」的意思。

hit below the belt │ 歹毒的，惡毒的

拳擊比賽是禁止攻擊腰帶 (belt) 以下的身體部位，因此攻擊人的胯下是相當不公平且陰狠的。

賭博（這算運動嗎？）

under the table │ 暗地裡

賭博時在桌子底下做的小動作，這當然是指「在暗地裡、檯面下做某件事」的意思囉。

give sb. a fair shake │ 公平對待

a fair shake 就是公平搖動骰子，因此引申為「給某人公平的機會」。

釣魚

off the hook │ 脫身

想像一下，自己像是掙脫魚鉤 (hook) 的魚，因此 off the hook 延伸有「脫離麻煩，擺脫責任」。

plenty of other fish in the sea
天涯何處無芳草

海裡還有其他許多魚，表示還有很多其他的選擇，其實就是中文的「天涯何處無芳草」，表示有很多可以找的對象啦。

其他

long shot │ 成功機率很低，不太可能發生

not by a long shot │ 差得遠了

這則片語的起源有幾個不同版本，最容易聯想到的版本是，十八到十九世紀初的火藥技術還不發達，遠距離射擊 (long shot) 的準度很低，因此此片語衍伸有「成功機率很低、難以達成的事」之意。另一個表現方式是 not by a long shot，意思為「差得遠；連絲毫機會都沒有」。

skate on thin ice｜身歷險境

在薄冰上滑冰 (skate)，意思就是「做危險或冒險的事」。

Tommy: Why haven't you asked Jenny out yet?
Bob: I'm not quite sure how she feels about me. I don't wanna jump the gun.
Tommy: Well, the ball is in your court, so it's now or never.

(after Bob asks Jenny out...)

Tommy: How did it go? Did she say yes?
Bob: Not by a long shot. She said I'm not her type.
Tommy: Not to take the wind out of your sails, but she is kind of out of your league.
Bob: Aren't you supposed to say something nice now?
Tommy: My bad, my bad. No worries! There's plenty of other fish in the sea.

湯米：你怎麼還沒約珍妮出去？
鮑伯：我不是很確定她對我的感覺怎麼樣，我不想要太倉促行動。
湯米：你知道的，主導權在你手上，不是現在就永遠沒機會了。

(鮑伯約珍妮後……)

湯米：怎麼樣？她有答應嗎？
鮑伯：差得遠了，她說我不是她的菜。
湯米：不是我要洩你的氣，不過她有點不是你高攀得起的。
鮑伯：你現在不是應該說些好話嗎？
湯米：我的錯，我的錯。別擔心！天涯何處無芳草？

Jack: Our new product launch is in full swing, and it's blowing the competition away.
Gina: Are you sure we can beat the market leader?
Jack: No sweat!

(after a couple weeks...)

Gina: I know what you've been doing under the table, Jack. You're skating on thin ice.
Jack: Listen to me, Gina. The regulations fall in a huge grey area. So technically speaking, we're not violating any laws.
Gina: No, Jack. You're playing with fire. We'll never get off the hook if anything goes wrong.

傑克：我們的新產品上市正在如火如荼進行中，而且徹底輾壓了其他競爭品牌。
吉娜：你確定我們可以超前市場領先者嗎？
傑克：絲毫不費力。

(幾個禮拜之後……)

吉娜：傑克，我知道你檯面下做了什麼，你這樣做太冒險了。
傑克：聽我的，吉娜，法令規章有很大的灰色地帶，所以技術上來說，我們並沒有違反任何法律。
吉娜：不，傑克，你這是在玩火，如果事情有任何差錯，我們都脫不了身的。

When you learn, you learn for a short time, however you use that learning for a lifetime.

學習時，只需要短時間就能學會，卻能使用一輩子。

—— 出自 JR 的筆記本

How I Learned

我的英文學習經歷

❶ native speaker

母語人士。母語是 **mother tongue** 或 **native language**，**My native language is Spanish.**（我的母語是西班牙語。）會講兩種語言的人叫做 **bilingual speaker**，可以說 **He's bilingual.**（他會講兩種語言。）會講三種語言則是 **trilingual**，四種語言以上的就稱呼 **multilingual**，或者直接說 **She speaks four languages.**（她會講四種語言。）

❷ ESL (English as a second language)

把英語當作第二語言來學習。也就是說除了母語之外，最常使用的就是英語，如香港就是 **ESL**。而臺灣則是屬於 **EFL**（**English as a foreign language**），指英語並非實際常用來溝通的語言，只在特殊目的才使用。

As I once mentioned in my most viewed YouTube video, the question I get asked most is, "How did you learn English?" And my response to that is, "Well, I grew up in the States." To be honest, I always feel [1]**reluctant** to talk about my language-learning background. On the one hand, I spent half of my childhood [2]**abroad**; on the other, I haven't lived in an English-speaking country since the fourth grade. At times I feel like I'm kind of stuck between being a ❶**native** and non-native English **speaker**.

Anyway, this is my story. I was born in Taiwan, and moved to America with my family when I was two years old. We moved back to Taiwan when I was ten, and I've been here ever since. After kindergarten, I was placed in ❷**ESL (English as a second language)** in first grade. Ms. Pinkawa—fingers crossed on spelling her name right—was really nice and helpful to me, and I fit in fast. In no time, I was speaking ❸**colloquial** English just like every other kid in class. Instead of worrying about my English, my parents were worried about my horrible Chinese. At first, they took me to Chinese class after school. I guess they gave up after a while since I hated it.

When I came back to Taipei after finishing third grade, in addition to the ❹**culture shock**, I [3]**had difficulty** reading, writing and speaking Chinese. My first school year in this "foreign land" was [4]**horrific**. It took me a whole year to [5]**catch up with my Chinese**. In this process, English became my seldom-spoken [6]**secondary** language, and kind of got left [7]**on the shelf** till high school. What's funny was that I didn't realize I could in fact speak pretty [8]**fluent** English. I had a hard time [9]**picking up** grammar, but somehow I always magically got all the

English

answers right. Well, nearly all of them. So to me, English was a subject that I didn't fully understand but somehow did okay at.

After not using the language [10]**on a regular basis** for years, my English did get a bit [11]**rusty**. And despite having the advantage of growing up abroad, I still had to [12]**expand** my vocabulary, do lots of reading and practice my speaking just like everyone else. In college, I wondered if I could learn a new language the way I did with English. So I picked up French—which, by the way, I've mostly forgotten already. Then I learned Korean. And I can tell you that [13]**at the end of the day**, there's no [14]**shortcut** to learning anything. That [15]**goes for** English, too.

※ 底線單字為「複習單字」，為之前出現過的字。

❸ **colloquial**

口語的，會話的。**That is not my money（那不是我的錢。）**是標準英文，如果用口語方式表達，可以說 **That ain't my money.** 有時候看一個人講話是否 **colloquial**，就可以推測對方是不是 **native speaker**「母語人士」。

....

❹ **culture shock**

文化衝擊，指接觸到不同人種、文化、思想時所受到的思想衝擊。

JR YouTube
影片 #12

雖然我在小學四年級之前有很好的語言基礎，但是直到現在，我每天還是需要花時間精進自己的語言實力，聽 Podcast、閱讀、記單字、做筆記。我也用一樣的態度和方法學習過法語和韓語。學習任何事物都一樣，只要付出努力，一定會有不同程度的收穫，**Tu peux le faire!** 힘내세요！

JR的話

How I Learned English
我的英文學習經歷

就像我在我 YouTube 頻道最多人觀看的影片裡所提到的一樣，我最常被問到的問題是：「你是怎麼學英文的？」我的回應都是：「這個嘛，我在美國長大的啊。」坦白說，我不太喜歡談自己的語言學習經歷。一方面，我的童年有一半都是在國外度過的，另一方面，我從國小四年級之後就不住在英美語系國家了。有時候，我覺得自己是介在母語跟非母語人士之間。

總之，我的故事是這樣的。我在臺灣出生，兩歲的時候跟家人搬到美國。我們在我十歲的時候搬回臺灣，從此就定居下來。幼稚園之後，我一年級去上英語為第二外語的課後班。Pinkawa 老師（希望我沒拼錯她的名字）人很親切，給我很多幫助，而我很快就適應了。沒多久，我就能跟班上其他同學們一樣講著口語的英文。比起擔心我的英文，我爸媽還比較煩惱我的破中文。一開始他們還讓我放學後上中文課。過了不久他們就放棄了，因為我實在是太討厭上課了。

我讀完三年級之後回到臺灣，除了受到文化衝擊之外，我在閱讀、書寫和說中文上都遇到困難。我在這片「異鄉之地」的第一年，只有糟透了可以形容。我花了一整年的時間補上中文程度。在這個過程中，英文變成我鮮少說出口的語言，上中學之前幾乎被我束之高閣。有趣的是，我其實沒有認知到我可以講出一口流利的英文。那時候我文法學得很痛苦，但不知為何，我總能神奇地答對所有的問題。嗯，幾乎啦。所以對當時的我而言，英文是一門我不太懂，但是不知為何成績還不錯的科目。

在好幾年沒有規律使用這個語言之後，我的英文確實變得有點生疏。即便有在國外長大的優勢，但我還是得跟其他人一樣，擴充單字量，大量閱讀，並且練習英文口說。上大學的時候，我想知道自己是否能像過去學英文一樣來學習另一門新語言，所以我學了法語。雖然我到現在已經忘得差不多了。接著我還學了韓語。而我現在可以告訴你，到頭來，學習任何事物都是沒有捷徑的。學英文也是。

Vocabulary & Phrases
單字片語

042

1. reluctant [rɪˋlʌktənt] *(adj.)* │ **勉強的，不情願的**

Jenny is reluctant to join the daily meetings because she finds them boring.
珍妮不情不願參加每天的會議，因為她覺得很無聊。

....

2. abroad [əˋbrɔd] *(adv.)* │ **在國外，到國外**

I lived in a dorm when I studied abroad and the food was horrible.
我在國外讀書時住宿舍，那裡的食物糟透了。

....

3. have difficulty (doing sth.) │ **（做某事）遇到困難**

近似 have a hard time (doing sth.)。

....

4. horrific [hɔˋrɪfɪk] *(adj.)* │ **極其可怕的；令人震驚的**

horrible 跟 horrific 都跟 horror「恐怖」有關，兩個都有「可怕的」意思，
而 horrific 在程度上比 horrible 更可怕。
不過 horrible 除了指「可怕的」，也指「糟透的，令人不愉快的」。

(Tommy and Gina have just watched a horror movie.)

Gina: Some of the scenes were so horrific. I couldn't even open my eyes.

Tommy: Really? I thought it was a snooze fest. I felt like leaving halfway through.

（湯米和吉娜去看了一場恐怖電影。）

吉娜：有些畫面實在太恐怖了，我都不敢睜開眼睛。

湯米：真的嗎？我無聊到快睡著了，看到一半就想走了。

* snooze fest │非常無聊的事物

5. catch up with sb. │ 趕上某人某事

這個片語的用途非常廣泛，除了本篇用法，也可以形容「被某事纏上（通常指以前發生的壞事）」，
如 His criminal past caught up with him.（他作奸犯科的過往終究找上了他。）
也可以用來說「待會再聊，待會再說」，如 I'll catch up with you later.（我晚點找你。）

She ran as fast as she could, but she couldn't catch up with her brother.
她使出全力地跑，但還是追不上她哥哥。

The new student had difficulty catching up with the rest of the class.
新進學生跟不上班上其他人（的進度）。

....

6. secondary [ˈsɛkən.dɛrɪ] (adj.) │ 次要的

Money is secondary to your health.
健康比金錢來得重要。

....

7. on the shelf │ 被擱置的

被放到書架上，意思就是「被忽視的，被擱置的」，類似中文的「束之高閣」，
經常會跟動詞 leave 或 put 一起使用。

The player suffered a knee injury that kept him on the shelf.
那名選手因膝蓋受傷所以無法上場。

....

8. fluent [ˈfluənt] (adj.) │（語言）流利的

相反地，要形容一個人講的語言很破，可以說 She speaks poor/bad French. 講話有口音則用 accent 這
個字，如 She speaks French with an/a heavy/a slight accent. 或 She has an accent.。

She is fluent in French.
她的法文很流利。
= She speaks fluent French.
= She speaks French fluently.
= She is a fluent French speaker.

....

9. pick sth. up │（透過練習）學會某事

10. on a regular basis │經常地，等同 regularly

也可以更換為 daily basis（每天）、weekly basis（每週）、monthly basis（每月），以此類推。

It's easy to pick up Spanish if you study on a regular basis.
如果你每天讀一點西班牙文，很快就能學起來。

......

11. rusty [ˋrʌstɪ] (adj.) │生鏽的；生疏的

rusty 原意是「生鏽的」，用在語言或做事上，就表示「在某方面生疏」。以前在 ICRT，就連外國 DJ 也會說他們在臺灣待久了，英文雖然不到生疏，但是有時會變得有點怪怪的（臺式英文），這時候他們會說 My English sounds a little off sometimes.（我的英文有時候聽起來有點怪怪的。）sound a little off 是「聽起來有點怪怪」的意思。

My French is a bit rusty.
我的法文有點生疏了。

......

12. expand [ɪkˋspænd] (v.) │展開，張開；擴張

Traveling abroad can really expand your horizons.
到國外旅行真的能夠擴展你的視野。

* **broaden/expand/widen one's horizons** │擴展視野，horizons 是「地平線」的意思。

......

13. at the end of the day │最終，到頭來

You can listen to whatever advice you like, but remember, at the end of the day, you are responsible for your own decisions.
你可以聽取任何人給的意見，但是請記得，到頭來你必須要對你自己做的決定負責。

......

14. shortcut [ˋʃɔrt.kʌt] (n.) │捷徑

走捷徑則會用 take a shortcut。

Tommy: I know a shortcut that'll save us 20 minutes.
Bob: Great. Maybe we'll be able to catch up with Jack.

湯米：我知道一條捷徑，可以幫我們省下二十分鐘。
鮑伯：太好了，這樣也許我們就可以追上傑克了。

15. the same/that goes for sb./sth. │ 同樣適用於某人事物，對某人事物來說也是如此

(Mom is talking to Charlie and his little brother.)

Mom: Charlie, how many times have I told you not to leave your stuff in the living room? And that goes for you too, young man.

（媽媽跟查理還有查理的弟弟講話。）

媽媽：查理，我跟你說了多少次，不要把你的東西放在客廳，小的，你也一樣！

正能量
座右銘
MOTTO

It doesn't matter where you come from, what you have or don't have, what you lack, or what you have too much of. But all you need to have is faith in God, an undying passion for what you do and what you choose to do in this life, and a relentless drive and the will to do whatever it takes to be successful in whatever you put your mind to.

你從哪裡來、擁有或沒有什麼、缺乏或具備過多的什麼,這些都無關緊要。你只需要對神有信心,對你做的事以及這輩子選擇所要從事的事物抱有不滅的熱情,還有為了成功不計一切代價的不間歇的動力和意志。

—— NBA 球星
Stephan Curry 史蒂芬柯瑞

I [1]Went the Extra M
Get My First Job

❶ enter the workforce

workforce 是「勞動力」，因此 enter the workforce 是指「進入職場」。另一個相關的單字是 workplace，更強調地點，指「工作場所，工作地點」。

❷ graduate

作動詞時是「畢業」，名詞指「畢業生」。undergraduate 是「（尚未畢業的）大學生」，graduate student 是「研究生」，千萬別搞混囉！美國大學每個年級還有不同的稱呼，不像中文講大一、大二……。從大一到大四依序是 freshman, sophomore, junior, senior。

❸ aim for the stars

或作 reach for the stars。想摘天上的星星，形容「追求難以實現的事物」。

❹ set the world on fire

不是要在世界縱火喔！而是形容「引起轟動，大獲成功」。

Before **❶entering the workforce**, I was a young, [2]**ambitious** **❷graduate** **❸aiming for the stars**. I wanted to **❹set the world on fire**, **❺make a dent in the universe**. So after completing my military service, I [3]**applied for** a job at a big international company.

My degree didn't meet the [4]**requirements** for the marketing position I wanted to apply for, so I applied for a sales job instead. After all, these days, no matter what position you're in, you're always selling something—a product, an idea, an opinion—to someone, right? So why not?

I knew the competition would be [5]**intense** when hundreds of **❻applicants** showed up for the first stage—the written exam. I hadn't even completed all the questions when the [6]**time was up**, so I had no expectations. To my surprise, I was [7]**notified** to come in for an interview.

I knew my [8]**chances were slim**, and I had to find a way to stand out. So I went the extra mile. I grabbed my camera and went to a retail store downtown. Immediately, I spotted something wrong in the promotion area, and I [9]**snapped a picture** of it. After I got home, I printed it out and wrote some notes at the bottom.

On interview day, I was greeted by a senior supervisor. It was an all-English interview, which I [10]**figured** would be [11]**in my favor**. [12]**Smirk**. I offered him my **❻résumé**, which he said they already have a copy of. "Well, I added a few more pages to it recently, just to let you know," I politely replied. The interview went on for 15 or 20 minutes, and right before we were about to [13]**wrap it up**, the manager [14]**flipped through** my files and stopped on the last page—where I placed the photo.

"Who told you to do this?" he asked. "No one," I replied. I just spotted the problem and thought I should [15]**bring it to your attention**." He smiled and thanked me for coming.

That wasn't the final stage, but a few months later I was hired. Only later did I find out that the man who interviewed me that day was [16]**in charge of** [17]**distribution** for that specific retail store. And I happened to [18]**point out** something worth improving there.

Call it a [19]**coincidence**, but I like to think that good luck only happens when you go the extra mile and do more than what's expected of you.

※ 底線單字為「複習單字」，為之前出現過的字。

❺ **make a dent in the universe**

dent 指「凹痕」，**make a dent in sth.** 有「在某事上取得進展，對某事產生影響」，所以想在宇宙敲出凹痕，意思就是「改變世界，影響世界」。

❻ **résumé**

簡歷，履歷。應徵工作時通常還需要以下文件：**cover letter**「求職信」，**academic transcript**「成績單」，**letter of recommendation**「推薦信」，**autobiography**「自傳」或 **bio**「個人經歷，小傳」。

JR 的話

我應徵生平第一份全職工作的經歷，讓我體會到，勤勞、努力、站在對方立場思考有多麼重要！當你肯付出辛勞，做出超乎對方期待的事，結果也會往往超出你的意料之外。

I Went the Extra Mile to
Get My First Job

付出多一點的努力
我得到第一份工作

中文翻譯

在踏進職場之前，我是個年輕、企圖心很強的畢業生，對未來充滿著願景和目標。我想要引起旋風、改變世界。所以我一服完兵役，就跑去一間大型國際企業應徵。

我的學歷不符合我想應徵的行銷職位的條件，所以我改應徵業務。畢竟在這個世代，不管你身處什麼職位，你總是在向某人、某團體推銷某樣東西——不管是一項商品、一個想法、或是一個意見。是吧？所以，何不這麼做呢？

當我看到數百名應徵者來參加第一關筆試時，我就知道競爭會相當激烈。筆試時間結束時，我連題目都寫不完，所以我自然也沒期待自己能進入下一關。然而，出乎我意料之外，我收到了面試通知。

我知道我的機會渺茫，我必須想辦法脫穎而出。於是我比我應該要做的多做了一點。我拿了我的相機，跑到市區的一家零售商店。我很快就注意到促銷陳列區怪怪的，便把它拍了下來。回到家之後，我把照片印出來，在底下寫了一些字。

到了面試當天，面試我的是一位資深主管。它是全英文面試，我心想這對我有利（竊笑）。我拿出履歷表給他，他說他們手上已經有一份了。我禮貌回應：「我最近增加了幾頁內容，只是讓你知道一下。」那場面試大概進行了15 到 20 分鐘，正當我們即將結束的時候，那名經理快速翻閱我的履歷，並在翻到最後一頁時停了下來。那正是我放那張照片的地方。

他問：「是誰告訴你這樣做的？」「沒有人叫我這樣做，」我回答，「我只是剛好看到這個問題，想說應該讓你們知道。」他微笑並感謝我來面試。

當天面試並不是最後一關。不過，幾個月之後，我錄取了。在那之後我才知道，那位面試我的人恰巧就是負責那間零售商店的鋪貨。而我正好點出了那裡應該要改善的地方。

你可以說是巧合。但我認為：好運只會發生在你做得更多一點，付出比預期更多一些的時候。

Vocabulary & Phrases
單字片語

※ 底線單字為「複習單字」，為之前出現過的字。

1. go the extra mile｜多付出一些，多努力一些

字面上的意思是多走一英里路，延伸有「付出比自己應該要或是別人期望中還要大的努力」。

Tommy's the kind of guy who would go the extra mile to help out a friend.
湯米是那種會為了幫助朋友而多做很多的人。

2. ambitious [æmˋbɪʃəs] *(adj.)*｜有抱負的，志向遠大的，野心勃勃的

3. requirement [rɪˋkwaɪrmənt] *(n.)*｜要求；必要條件

If you're an ambitious person with an interest in sales, please send us your résumé and salary requirements.
如果你富有企圖心且對業務工作有興趣，請將你的履歷和薪資需求寄給我們。

4. apply [əˋplaɪ] *(v.)*｜申請

慣用說法是 apply for sth. 或 apply to do sth.，名詞是 application。至於「申請人」則是 applicant。

You need a copy of your birth certificate to apply for a passport.
你需要提供出生證明才能申請護照。

5. intense [ɪnˋtɛns] *(adj.)*｜強烈的，劇烈的

Bob felt an intense pain in his stomach right before going to work this morning.
今天早上鮑伯出門上班前感到肚子一陣劇痛。

6. time's up ｜（口語）時間到了

Time's up. Please <u>hand in</u> your exam papers.
時間到了，請交卷。

---

7. notify [ˋnotəˏfaɪ] *(v.)* ｜通知，告知

Jack:	Bob is calling in sick today. He notified HR this morning.
Tommy:	I guess I'm gonna have to <u>cover</u> for him today.

傑克：鮑伯今天請病假，他早上有告知人力資源部。
湯米：看來今天我得頂替他的工作了。

* **call in sick** ｜（打電話）請病假

---

8. chances are slim ｜機會渺茫

Jack:	Do you think the clients will accept our <u>offer</u>?
Tommy:	I think the chances are slim. I heard our competitor gave a much lower quote.

傑克：你覺得客戶會接受我們的提案嗎？
湯米：我覺得機會渺茫，聽說我們的競爭者開出的報價超低。

* **quote** [kwot] *(n.)* ｜報價

---

9. snap a picture/photo ｜（口語）快速拍下照片

I was staying at the same hotel as Tom Cruise during my vacation, and I managed to snap a picture of him.
我度假時剛好跟湯姆克魯斯住同一家飯店，而且我還設法拍了一張他的照片。

---

10. figure [ˋfɪg(j)ə] *(v.)* ｜認為，以為

We figured you might be worried about your project while you were on sick leave, so we finished it for you.
我們想說你在病假期間可能會擔心你的專案，所以我們就幫你做完了。

* **sick leave** ｜病假

11. in one's favor | 對某人有利

也可以說 in favor of sb.。

I'm so relieved that the <u>court</u> ruled in my favor!
法院判決對我有利，我整個壓力都解除了！

. . . .

12. smirk [sm3k] *(v.)/(n.)* | 得意地笑，詭異地笑

Jack:	What are you smirking about?	傑克：你在竊笑什麼？
Tommy:	We got the deal! The other company backed out at the last minute.	湯米：我們拿到合約了！另一間公司最後一刻退出了。
Jack:	Really? Well wipe that smirk off your face 'cause we're gonna have to burn the midnight oil to meet the deadline.	傑克：真的假的？那還不趕快收起你詭異的笑容，這下我們要熬夜趕在截止日期前完工了。

* **back out** | 退出

* **burn the midnight oil** | 日以繼夜地工作或念書

. . . .

13. wrap it up | （口語）結束工作或會議

It looks like we've <u>covered</u> everything, so I guess it's time to wrap up the meeting.
看來我們已經討論完所有議題，我想差不多該結束會議了。

. . . .

14. flip through | 快速翻閱

Shelly flipped through a magazine while she was waiting at the dentist's office.
雪莉在牙醫診所等候時，翻閱了一本雜誌。

. . . .

15. bring sth. to one's attention | 使某人注意某事

. . . .

16. be in charge of | 負責

I'm in charge of this department, so if you encounter a problem, please bring it to my attention.
我負責這個部門，如果你有遇到問題，請讓我知道。

17. distribution [ˌdɪstrəˈbjuʃən] *(n.)* | 分發，分配

在商業上則是「鋪貨；配貨」，distributor 則是「經銷商」，動詞則為 distribute。

---

18. point sth. out | 點出某事

尤其是指提出對方不知道的某件事。

Daniel pointed out that there were still serious distribution <u>issues</u> that needed to be solved.
丹尼爾指出，部分嚴重的配貨問題仍有待解決。

---

19. coincidence [koˈɪnsɪdəns] *(n.)* | 巧合

形容詞是 coincidental。

Gina:	I went to sign up for a gym membership today. Guess who I saw there? Jenny!
Tommy:	Wow, what a coincidence!

吉娜：我今天去加入了健身房會員，你猜我在那遇到誰？珍妮！
湯米：哇，怎麼那麼巧！

* sign up | 報名參加

正能量
座右銘
MOTTO

Wherever you go, don't let the environment affect you, don't let your surroundings limit you. Live your life like a clock.

不論你去到哪裡，別讓環境影響你，別讓周遭的事物限制了你。像時鐘一樣地生活。

—— 出自 JR 的筆記本

Live Like a Cl

像時鐘一樣生活

❶ make things/matters worse

情況更糟的是……，雪上加霜的是……。指原本狀況就很糟，但卻又發生更多事情讓狀況更加嚴峻。

....

❷ put oneself in... position

position 有「處境、狀況」的意思，把自己放到什麼處境，言下之意就是「讓自己處於……狀況；讓自己身陷……處境」。

....

❸ lose one's head (over sth.)

失控。字面翻譯是失掉自己的頭，意思就是「因為某事而失去冷靜，或情緒失控」。

Everyone has had a time in their life when they feel lost and confused. Mine was when I decided to leave my first job. It was a couple years since I'd entered the workforce, and I was ¹**having second thoughts** about my career path. I felt like I was slowly ²**drifting away** from my original ³**motivation**—my desire to change the world. And when I asked myself where I saw myself in ten years, I didn't have a satisfying answer.

And so I made an ⁴**audacious** move—I quit my ⁵**lucrative** job. I even ⁶**doubled down** by turning down other job offers in the same industry. This, however, came with a heavy price. I was ⁷**acting on** a ⁸**vague** idea about "changing the world." Maybe I was too ⁹**naïve**. That's what I got a lot from the people around me. And soon, **❶to make things worse**, I was ¹⁰**running low on** cash. I **❷put myself in a position** where I cut off my financial sources, where nobody believed in me, and where I began to lose faith in myself.

By the time it seemed as if all hope was lost, I ¹¹**by chance** read an open letter written by a pastor. In it, I was struck by the following passage: "You need to live your life like a clock. Because no matter where you put it, in good or bad environment, the clock will keep ticking without missing a beat."

I was deeply inspired by these words. I could either be **❸losing my head over things** I don't have control over, or prepping myself for the future despite the current uncertainty. Within a few days, I came up with a detailed daily plan based on the skills and ¹²**traits** I needed in order to get closer to my goal of "changing the world." I ¹³**dug in** and followed my daily routine, regular as clockwork. Some 18 months after quitting my job, I was hired by a major radio station, where I **❹found my voice** on the air.

※ 底線單字為「複習單字」，為之前出現過的字。

❹ find one's voice

什麼叫做找到自己的聲音呢？就是「能夠按照自己所想，表達自己的想法、點子、主張」。我在本篇文章所提到 **found my voice on the air** 則是玩雙關語，**on (the) air** 是「廣播放送中」，因此這句既是「在廣播上找到我的聲音」，也是「在廣播上得以表達我的想法」的意思。

JR YouTube
影片 #13

處於低潮中的自己並不代表是真正的自己。但是在艱困的時刻中，自己選擇如何面對，則會定義你將成為什麼樣的人。這是我在最辛苦的時候，所學到最寶貴的一課。

Live Like
a Clock

像時鐘
一樣生活

每個人都曾有過迷失與困惑的人生時期。我也有，那正是我決定離開我第一份工作的時候。那是我進入職場之後幾年發生的事，當時我正在重新思考我的職涯。我覺得自己正在偏離初衷 —— 偏離我想改變世界的欲望。當我捫心自問，十年後的自己會是怎麼樣，我找不到令自己滿意的答案。

所以我做了一個大膽的決定 —— 我辭掉了薪資優渥的工作。我吃了秤砣鐵了心，拒絕了同一個業界內的其他工作機會。然而，這個舉動讓我付出沉重的代價。我所謂「改變世界」的想法其實非常模糊。也許我太過天真了，至少我周遭的親友都是這樣跟我說的。很快地，雪上加霜的是，我的積蓄幾乎見底了。我讓自己深陷在一個沒有經濟收入、沒有人相信我的處境中。而我也開始對自己失去信心。

就在一切看似了無希望的時候，我在因緣際會之下，讀到一位牧師寫的公開信。我讀到下面這一段時受到了衝擊：「你要把你的生命活得像時鐘一樣。因為，無論你將時鐘放在好的或壞的環境中，它依然是分毫不差地繼續走下去。」

我深深受到這段文字的啟發。我大可以因著那些我無法控制的事情而發慌，但我也可以積極準備自己好迎接未來，即便是在眼前充滿不確定性的現實之中。為了更接近我所謂「改變世界」的目標，我依照我所需要增進的技能與特質，在接下來幾天內想出了一個鉅細彌遺的每日計畫。像是時鐘一般，我下了莫大的決心，規律實行了我的每日例行計畫。在我辭職 18 個月之後，我被一間大廣播公司錄取，在廣播上找到了自己的聲音。

Vocabulary & Phrases
單字片語

※ 底線單字為「複習單字」，為之前出現過的字。

---

1. have second thoughts │ 猶豫；重新考慮

I'm starting to have second thoughts about quitting my job now. Jobs aren't easy to find nowadays.
我開始猶豫要不要辭職，畢竟現在工作難找。

---

2. drift away │ 飄走；偏離

---

3. motivation [ˌmotɪˋveʃən] (n.) │ 動機；誘因

Without strong motivation, it's easy to drift away from your goals.
沒有強烈的動機，你會容易離你的目標越來越遠。

---

4. audacious [ɔˋdeʃəs] (adj.) │ 大膽的，敢於冒險的；魯莽的

It was an audacious move to sub in the young player in the final minutes of the game when we were still trailing.
在比賽剩下最後幾分鐘、我們還處於落後之際，換上那位年輕球員真的是很大膽的行動。

* sub in │（體育比賽中）替補上位。替補下場則說 sub out。

---

5. lucrative [ˋlukrətɪv] (adj.) │ 賺錢的；有利可圖的

As lucrative as show biz may seem, only a handful of people make the big money.
演藝圈看似可以賺大錢，但是真正做到的人只有少數。

* a handful of │ 一隻手可以抓的量，意思是「少數的；少量的」。

6. double down (on sth.) ｜加倍努力（做某事）

原本是用在玩撲克牌二十一點時，看完前兩張牌之後決定加倍下注，
衍伸為「強化決心毅力；加倍付出」。

Although his last album went under the radar, the singer is doubling down by releasing his new album out of his own pocket.
儘管這位歌手上一張專輯乏人問津，他還是決定賭下去自掏腰包出新專輯。

* **under/below the radar** ｜沒有被雷達（radar）偵測到，意思就是「未被注意到」。
* **out of one's own pocket** ｜自掏腰包

7. act on/upon sth. ｜採取行動

除了指根據自己想法採取行動之外，也可以用在受到別人的建議或他人命令而行動。

The government is acting on incomplete information they've received from abroad.
政府當局是根據從國外所收到的不完整訊息來採取行動。

8. vague [veg] (adj.) ｜模糊不清的，不明確的，含糊的

I have a vague memory of meeting him many years ago.
我依稀記得幾年前有見過他。

9. naïve [nɑˋiv] (adj.) ｜天真的，輕信的；幼稚的（通常是負面的）

Tommy: Is there any chance Jack would let us work at home once a week?

Bob: Don't be naïve! You know what he's like.

湯米：傑克有沒有可能讓我們一個禮拜在家工作一天？

鮑伯：別天真了！你知道他的為人。

10. run low on (sth.) ｜缺少、快用完（某物）

類似用法有 be short of sth.。

We're running low on gas. I hope there's a gas station nearby.
我們快沒油了，希望附近有加油站。

11. by chance │ 意外地，偶然

The couple met by chance at a school dance.
那對情侶是偶然間在學校舞會認識的。

....

12. trait [tret] (n.) │ 個人特質

What kinds of personality traits are they looking for in their new recruits?
他們想在新員工身上找到什麼樣的人格特質？

* recruit [rɪˋkrut] (n.) │ 新成員

....

13. dig in (to sth.) │ 帶著極大的決心（開始做某事）

不過，dig in 也有「（口語）盡量吃；開始吃吧」的意思。

It's time to dig in and prepare for our big presentation.
該開始準備我們的重大簡報。

More Expressions

Workplace 職場相關用語

24-7 (adj.) / (adv.) | **全年無休**

一天二十四小時，一個禮拜七天，意思就是「全年無休」。

around-the-clock (adj.) | **日以繼夜**

繞著時鐘跑一圈，意思就是「日以繼夜」。

from day one | **打從一開始**

I've been working around-the-clock from day one since our clients' stores are open 24-7.

我從上班第一天開始就沒日沒夜地工作，
因為我們客戶的店面是 24 小時全年無休的。

put sth. off | **延期**

call sth. off | **取消**

the eleventh hour | **最後一刻，最後關頭**

第十一個小時，延伸有「最後一刻，最後關頭」之意。

Why did you have to wait until the eleventh hour to call off the meeting? You could have announced it earlier!

你為什麼非要等到最後一刻才取消會議？
你明明可以早點宣布的！

call it a day | **今天到此結束**

字面上意思就是「今天就到這裡！」表示今天的工作或上課就到此為止。

All right, let's call it a day!

好吧，我們今天就到這裡結束！

get down to business | **談正事吧**

從一個輕鬆、休閒的狀態轉換到談正事的時候，就會說 Let's get down to business.。

the big picture | **大局**

大的畫面是什麼呢？就是「大局，整體概況」的意思。

the bottom line | **重點，關鍵**

We've been working our butts off, but the bottom line is we haven't been seeing the big picture.

我們過去不斷在賣肝工作，
但重點是我們一直沒有看到整體狀況。

in a nutshell | 簡而言之，總括來說

in conclusion | 最後

conclusion 是「結論」，in conclusion 就表示「最後」。
jump to conclusions 則表示「匆匆下結論」。

....

In conclusion, we will not be putting the press conference off for another week. In a nutshell, it's time to speed things up!

最後，記者會不會再延後一週。簡單來說，是該加快速度了！

take off | 事業起飛

take off 有「飛機起飛」的意思，也指「（事業、知名度等）起飛很快」的意思。

back to the drawing board | 從頭來過

back to the drawing board（繪圖板），表示計畫失敗要重新繪圖，因此就是「（因為失敗、行不通）重新開始；回到起始點」，跟 back to square one 類似。

**from the ground up
從零開始，從頭開始**

**get sth. off the ground
啟動、開始活動或事業**

back to square one | 從零開始

以前用收音機聽美式足球賽廣播，播報員會把場地劃分成好幾個格（square），在自家主場門前就叫做 square one，所以 back to square one 就是「從頭再來過；回到起始狀態」的意思。

test the waters | 試水溫

也就是在正式採取行動之前，詢問或試探對方反應。

....

It's a good thing we tested the waters before launching the product. Now sales are really taking off!

幸好我們在新產品上市前有先試水溫，現在銷售數字真的在起飛！

go down the drain | 心血、金錢等白費

go down（掉到）the drain（排水管），多可惜啊！所以意思就是「（金錢、心血等）被浪費掉，白費」。

....

I've built this project from the ground up, and I'd hate to see it go down the drain. But the market trends have changed since then, so we have to go back to the drawing board.

這項專案是我從零開始打造的，我很不想看著它白費。但是市場趨勢已經改變，我們必須要重新開始。

behind the scenes │ 幕後

Jenny has been putting in a lot of hard work behind the scenes, so I believe she can bring valuable experience to the table.

珍妮在幕後付出許多努力，我相信她可以帶來寶貴的經驗。

cut corners │ 走捷徑；偷工減料

想像一下，開車轉彎時，為了求快而切過（cut）轉角（corners），所以延伸有「（為了省錢省事）走捷徑，偷工減料」。

Our suppliers have been cutting corners. That's why the defect rate is so high.

我們的供應商偷工減料，這就是為什麼不良率這麼高。

bring sth. to the table
為某個計畫、討論帶來貢獻

put / leave something on the back burner │ （因不重要）暫時擱在一旁

煮飯時，把某一鍋東西放在後方的爐子（back burner），表示那不是最重要的，所以延伸有「將某事擱置，待晚點處理」之意。

There's still some grey areas that need clarifying. Let's leave the plan on the back burner and come back to it later.

計畫還有一些灰色地帶需要釐清，我們先擱著，晚點再回來處理。

個人工作相關

by the book │ 按規定行事，依法行事

做什麼都照著書上寫的做，意思就是「按照規定、規矩做事」。

follow up │ 跟進

中文沒有完全對應的詞，一般在外商公司也會直接講 follow up，「採取進一步行動」的意思。名詞則是 follow-up(s)。

think outside the box
跳脫框架來思考

People, we're launching a new product. We can't be doing everything by the book. We need to improvise, think outside the box. Does anyone have any ideas? Anything off the top of your head?

各位，我們要上市新產品，不能夠照本宣科，必須要即興、在框架外思考，有人有任何點子嗎？任何你現在想得到的？

run around in circles｜瞎忙一場

原地兜圈子是什麼意思呢？表示「花費很多力氣，卻徒勞無功」。

have a lot on one's plate
要操心的事情很多

盤子（plate）裡裝了很多食物，衍伸為「有許多問題或工作要處理」；have a lot on one's mind 則是「心中有很多煩惱」。

....

Sorry that I didn't follow up on that email you sent me. I've got a lot on my plate and it has me running around in circles.

很抱歉我沒跟上你寄給我的電子郵件。
我上週太多事情要忙了，搞得我團團轉。

財務、數字相關

on a shoestring (budget)
金錢、資源或預算短缺

pennies on the dollar｜相當便宜

用 pennies（幾分美金）來買價值 dollar（一塊美金）的東西，顯然是一個很好的交易。因此，這個片語的意思是「用非常便宜的價格買」。

....

The charity is on a shoestring budget, but managed to buy much needed medical supplies for pennies on the dollar.

該慈善機構預算短少，不過他們設法用低廉價格買進必需的醫療供給品。

do the math｜好好斟酌、評估

可不是真的叫你算數學（math）喔！當別人叫你 do the math，通常在暗示你「答案很明顯了」，要你「自己斟酌評估看看」。

....

She hasn't been answering your calls or your texts. Do the math, bro. She's dumping you.

她不接你電話，也不回你電話，兄弟，你自己想一想吧，她要把你給甩了。

Other than the cost of car itself, you have to pay taxes and insurance. And gas prices are skyrocketing. Do the math—it's not worth buying a car.

除了車子本身，你還得繳稅金、買保險，更不用說油價狂漲，自己算一算吧，買車划不來啦。

crunch (the) numbers｜做大量數學計算

bang for the buck | 物美價廉，CP 值高

如果某件事為每一塊美金 (buck) 所帶來的聲響（bang) 很大，那就表示「單位效益很大」。因此，意思就是「花的錢很值得」，類似我們常說的「CP 值很高」。

....

Compared to radio ads, social media ads are <u>definitely</u> providing more bang for the buck these days.

比起廣播廣告，這年頭社群媒體廣告（每單位金錢）所帶來的效益是更大的。

workaholic (n.) | 工作狂

perfectionist (n.) | 完美主義者

people person | 人緣好、善於交際的人

team player | 善於團隊合作的人

have a say in sth. | 對某事有發言權

不是有話想說喔！按字面是「在某件事上有發言權」，意味著「可以實際影響或決定某事」。

....

Jenny's a real people person. Even though she's not <u>in charge of</u> the team, she <u>definitely</u> has a say in every thing going around here.

珍妮人緣真的很好，即便她不負責這個團隊，但這裡的大小事情都絕對會有人聽她說話。

touch base (with sb.) | (跟某人) 聯絡

....

We need to follow up on the promotion plan. I'll touch base with our client later.

我們必須跟進促銷計畫的進度。我晚點會跟客戶聯絡。

People can't do something themselves, they want to tell you you can't do it. If you want something, go get it. Period.

當人們自己做不到那件事情，就會跟你說你做不到。如果你有想達成的事，去做就對了。句點。

——電影
The Pursuit of Happyness《當幸福來敲門》

No One Believ

沒有人相信我

❶ freeway

高速公路。另一個容易搞混的字是 highway，這個字裡有一個「高（high）」，但事實上 highway 是指「公路」，特別是指連結州與州、城市與城市之間的公路，有點類似臺灣的「省道」。

❷ interchange

交流道。另一個容易搞混的單字是 intersection。字首 inter- 有「互相、兩者之間」的意思，所以 interchange 可以理解成，在高速公路和平面道路之間（inter）轉變（change），也就是「交流道」，如 We need to turn left at the next interchange.（我們要在下一個交流道左轉。）。而在一個區域（section）內相交則可以理解為「十字路口」，至少 JR 我當初是這麼記憶的啦！

One of the stories I'll never forget happened when me and two of my friends went to summer camp together one year. When I got to the [1]**campsite**, I had a hard time [2]**convincing** my friends, who had taken a taxi, that I'd run all the way there from the ❶**freeway** ❷**interchange**, a distance of nearly four kilometers.

"It took us ten minutes to get here by taxi! There's no way you could have run all the way here!" my friend said [3]**incredulously**. So I turned to my other friend and tried to [4]**persuade** her instead. Right away, the first friend grabbed her by the wrist and said, "Don't trust him. He's such a [5]**prankster**! Look how weak and [6]**scrawny** he is." I guess I may have [7]**gone too far** playing pranks on them once or twice before. And I am kind of skinny to be fair. There was no chance they were going to [8]**take me seriously**.

[9]**For the record**, I *did* run to campsite that day. In fact, it was [10]**easy-peasy** for someone who plays on a soccer team! The main reason they didn't believe me, I think, was simply because they probably couldn't do it themselves. So the joke's on them! By the way, I hope we're still friends if they ever [11]**get around to** reading my book. Wink.

In the 2006 movie ❸***The Pursuit of Happyness***, Chris Gardner, played by Will Smith, says to his son, "People can't do something themselves, they want to tell you you can't do it. If you want something, go get it. Period." Talk about [12]**motivational**!

People can only understand things to the level of their own knowledge, [13]**capabilities** and imagination. When people tell you, "You can't," it's

[14]**literally** them saying to you, "I can't, and therefore I can't picture you achieving it either." Don't [15]**take it personally** or be in a rush to [16]**defend** yourself. Just realize that that's the way people are. The best way to prove yourself is to put in the hard work and let your actions [17]**speak for themselves**. Just like the Wright brothers. No one believed they could fly, so they touched the sky.

※ 底線單字為「複習單字」，為之前出現過的字。

❸ *The Pursuit of Happyness*

2006 年電影《當幸福來敲門》是根據真實故事拍攝，由威爾史密斯（Will Smith）父子檔主演，劇情是真實世界主角 Chris Gardner 從帶著兒子流落街頭到逆轉人生的故事，電影在當年大受好評，威爾史密斯也因此被提名奧斯卡及金球獎最佳男主角。

片名的 Happiness 刻意寫錯成 Happyness，則是來自 Chris 的親身經驗，他人生最低潮的時候，他兒子托育中心的壁畫正是寫著 Happyness，而電影中也有出現這個場景喔！在訪問中他本人說明：「y 是代表『你』和『你的幸福』的意思。」

JR YouTube
影片 #14

本身是跆拳道黑段的瑞典足球明星 Zlatan Ibrahimović，曾經準確預言，2018 年的 UFC 重點格鬥賽事，Khabib Nurmagomedov 會在跟 Conor McGregor 的對決中勝出，他說：「Khabib 比較安靜（相較之下 Conor 總是娛樂性十足的垃圾話滿天飛），但我感覺他比較具有威脅性。」在生活中也是如此，我們無法強求要取信於人，但你永遠要用行動來為自己的話背書，行動是最牢不可破的證明。

JR的話

No One Believed Me
沒有人相信我

發生在我身上最令人難忘的一件事情,是我和兩位好友有一年去參加夏令營的事。我抵達營區時,花了好些力氣說服我那兩個搭了計程車過來的朋友,說我剛從高速公路交流道跑了快四公里來到營區。

「我們搭小黃過來就花了 10 分鐘耶!你不可能用跑的過來的!」我朋友一副不可置信的口氣。所以我決定轉而說服我另一個朋友。不過,第一個朋友立刻抓住她的手腕說:「妳不要相信他!他這麼愛騙人,妳看,他瘦得像皮包骨一樣,怎麼可能。」我想我之前可能有一兩次跟她們玩笑開過了頭。而且,她講得也沒錯,我的確是有點瘦。反正,她們就是完全不把我的話當一回事。

在此把話說清楚,我那天確實是跑步到營區的。事實上,這對加入足球隊的我來說輕而易舉。他們之所以不相信我,我想,就單純只是因為她們自己做不到。所以呢,這下換成她們糗大了。對了,如果有一天她們有機會讀到這本書,希望我們還是朋友。眨眼。

2006 年上映的電影《當幸福來敲門》裡頭,威爾史密斯飾演的克里斯,向自己兒子說:「當人們自己做不到那件事情,就會跟你說你做不到。如果你有想達成的事,去做就對了。句點。」真是激勵人心啊!

人只能理解自己知識、能力以及想像範圍內的事情。當別人告訴你:「你做不到。」他們其實是在說:「我做不到,所以我也無法想像你做得到。」別把這句話當成是針對你自己,別急著為自己辯解。只要明白一件事:會這麼想是人之常情。證明自己最棒的作法,是努力並且讓你的行動為你自己說話。就像發明飛機的萊特兄弟一般。沒人相信他們能飛,於是他們就觸碰到天際了。

Vocabulary & Phrases
單字片語

※ 底線單字為「複習單字」，為之前出現過的字。

1. campsite [ˋkæmp.saɪt] *(n.)* │ **營地**

2. convince [kənˋvɪns] *(v.)* │ **說服，使人信服**

Jenny:	I'm <u>having a hard time</u> believing what the fitness trainer said about losing weight in three days.
Gina:	Same here. He didn't convince me either.

珍妮：我不太相信健身教練講三天內減重的事。
吉娜：我也是。他講的也無法說服我。

3. incredulously [ɪnˋkrɛdʒələsli] *(adv.)* │ **不願相信地；表示懷疑地**

4. persuade [pɚˋswed] *(v.)* │ **說服；力勸**

那 persuade 跟 convince 有什麼差別呢？convince 是在心理上讓人信服、相信，
而 persuade 則是用外在的方式說服某人做某事。

The harder I tried to persuade her, the more incredulously she looked at me.
我越是努力想要說服她，她就越是用懷疑的眼神看著我。

5. prankster [ˋpræŋkstɚ] *(n.)* │ **惡作劇的人；愛胡鬧、開玩笑的人**

還記得前面文章有提到 prank 是「惡作劇」的意思嗎？所以這裡的 prankster 就是指「惡作劇的人」。

6. scrawny [ˋskrɔnɪ] *(adj.)* │ **瘦巴巴的；骨瘦如柴的**

Looking at Brad's muscles, it's hard to imagine he was scrawny as a kid.
看著布萊德的肌肉，很難想像他小時候是瘦巴巴的。

7. go too far │ 做過頭，做得太過分

指尺度沒有拿捏好，不小心踩了對方底線。

Jack went too far when he called Bob useless.
傑克說鮑伯很沒用是有點過頭了。

....

8. take sb./sth. seriously │ 認真看待某人某事

You should take me more seriously when I tell you to be on time.
當我叫你要遵守時間，你應該要認真地聽進去。

* on time │ 準時

....

9. for the record │ 鄭重聲明

按照字面意思是指為了正確地記錄，其實就是「鄭重聲明；公開說明」。
類似的片語則有 **set the record straight**「陳述真相、澄清真相」。
相反的片語則是 **off the record**「私下說；非正式聲明」。

For the record, I hate rice burgers. Don't ever ask me to eat one.
我要鄭重聲明，我討厭米漢堡，千萬不要叫我吃。

....

10. easy-peasy [ˋizi ˋpizɪ] *(adj.)* │（口語）簡單得很；容易極了

That sudoku was easy-peasy. Give me a harder one.
那個數獨謎題超級簡單的，來點難一點的。

....

11. get around to (do sth.) │ 抽空（做某事）

....

12. motivational [ˌmotɪˋveʃənəl] *(adj.)* │ 激勵人心的

After listening to JR's motivational speech, I finally got around to cleaning my apartment.
聽了 JR 激勵人心的演講之後，我終於抽空打掃了公寓。

13. capability [ˌkepəˋbɪlətɪ] (n.) │ 能力，才能，能耐

Who do you think has the capability to take on this assignment?
你認為誰有足夠的能力承接這項工作？

* **take on** │ 接受（挑戰）；承擔（責任）

....

14. literally [ˋlɪtərəlɪ] (adv.) │ 字面上來看；真的，確實如此

原意就是指「按照字面地」，延伸有「如字面上的意思一般，事情就是這樣子」，沒有話中有話。
這又是一個很難用中文解釋的字，看例句吧！

I literally fell asleep in the middle of the meeting.
我真的（就如同我字面上所說的）就開會到一半睡著了。

(Jenny is about to step on stage for a performance.)	（在珍妮上舞臺表演前。）
Gina: Break a leg out there!	**吉娜：**摔斷腿祝好運啊！
Jenny: Ooh, don't say that. I literally broke my leg on stage when I was little.	**珍妮：**哎呀，不要這麼說。我小時候真的在舞臺上摔斷過腿。

* **break a leg** │ 摔斷腿，這句話是在別人上舞臺表演前用來祝福好運的話。這裡尷尬的是，珍妮小時候真的在舞臺上摔斷腿過，所以珍妮此時用 literally，表達「按照妳字面上的意思，我真的摔斷過腿」，這樣有比較懂 literally 的用法了嗎？

....

15. take sth. personally │ 認為某事是針對自己的

Don't take it personally, but you literally smell like stinky tofu.
我不是要針對你喔，但是你真的聞起來就像臭豆腐一樣。

....

16. defend [dɪˋfɛnd] (v.) │ 辯護，辯解

Why are you always defending his bad behavior?
你幹嘛老是幫他的壞行為辯解啊？

....

17. sth. speaks for itself │ 不言自明

字面上的意思是「某事會為了自己說話」，其實就是「不言自明」，表示無需多說，
直接用某事證明自己。

Jack's excellent performance on the project speaks for itself.
傑克在專案上的優秀表現不需要多加說明了。

A pessimist sees the difficulty in every opportunity; an optimist sees the opportunity in every difficulty.

悲觀的人在機會中看見困難；樂觀的人則在困難中看見機會。

——前英國首相
Winston Churchill 邱吉爾

This Girl Reminded How I Could be Cha

❶ stage name

藝名。其他有關名字的字有 **nickname** 和 **moniker**，都指「綽號」，但是語感上稍有差異，**nickname** 常用在親人朋友之間，而 **moniker** 則是來自本人的某個特質或專長，如 Kobe Bryant 自稱 **Black Mamba**，雖然兩者都適用，但用 **moniker** 更適合。至於經常看到的 **AKA** 是什麼？它是 **also known as**「也稱之為」的縮寫。**alter ego** 則指「分身」，如碧昂絲提到她在舞臺上進入另一個狀態時，她的分身 **Sasha Fierce** 就會進場，真神奇！

....

❷ DJ

DJ 是 **disk jockey** 的縮寫，可指廣播電臺主持人或夜店刷盤放音樂的人。為了區分，分別會用 **radio DJ/ host** 以及 **club DJ**。

Early 2009 was a big ¹**turning point** in my life. ²**Against all odds**, I got my <u>break</u> in radio, starting as a weekend <u>host</u> at ICRT—Taiwan's only English language station. That's where I got my ❶**stage name**: JR.

In a year's time, I went from <u>hosting</u> weekend shows to hosting weekday noontime shows. My career was ³**blossoming**, and I was enjoying one of the best times of my life.

In 2012, the station gave all the DJs a new task. In addition to our <u>regular</u> programs, we each had to develop our own late night program, which would ⁴**air** once a week at midnight. It had to be something unique and different from the daytime shows. And while my fellow ❷**DJs** were ⁵**coming up with** great concepts involving ❸**indie music**, night club remixes, heavy metal and so on, I was kind of ⁶**strapped for** ideas. "What can I bring to my show that will ⁷**differentiate me from the other DJs**?" I wondered. Since I was the "good kid" at the station who went to church every Sunday, I eventually came up with the idea of creating an ⁸**uplifting** spiritual music program. I named the show "Skylight After Midnight", representing the idea of having hope even in the darkest time of night.

The show was all uplifting music and inspirational talk, something I really enjoyed doing. But even so, I wondered, "Is this really <u>making a dent in the universe</u>?" My late night listeners were less than ❹**a third** of my daytime <u>audience</u>. And unable to see my audience, it always felt like talking to a lone mic in a ⁹**solitary** room. "Am I really <u>reaching out to</u> anybody at all?" I wondered.

Me of
ging the World

這位女孩讓我明白
其實我正在改變世界

And then one day I received a message from a girl named Jenny. Jenny had just been accepted to college and was writing to tell me how much she'd enjoyed listening to "Skylight After Midnight" during her senior year of high school. Every Tuesday night, she would tune in while staying up late studying for exams. Jenny told me it helped [10]**lift her spirits** throughout the tough school year, and [11]**had a** life-changing **impact on** her afterwards. Included with her message was an attachment—a photo of all the notes she took while listening to my show.

To this very day, I still remind myself with this story of how I could be potentially influencing people with the tiny things I do. Little by little, person by person, heart by heart, we might not be able to save the world, but we can certainly change it.

※ 底線單字為「複習單字」，為之前出現過的字。

❸ indie music

indie 是「獨立製作」，indie music 就是「獨立音樂」，指由非主流音樂廠牌所製作的音樂。

....

❹ a/one third

三分之一；英文分數的講法有兩種，第一種是分母從 2 開始，依序說 half、third、fourth (quarter)、fifth、sixth、seventh 以此類推。當分子大於 2，分母的說法就要用複數，舉例來說，1/4 是 one-fourth (或 one quarter)，3/4 是 three-fourths (或 three quarters)。那麼 2 又 7/19 怎麼說呢？答案是 two and seven-nineteenths，懂了嗎？

JR 的話

我經常聽到臺上的牧師們講的一句話是：「不要忘記過去的故事。這麼一來，信心就不會觸礁。」這些日子以來，我始終沒有忘記這句話，每當我信心低落的時候，我會想起當年在廣播電臺所發生的故事。

This Girl Reminded Me of
How I Could be Changing the World

這位女孩讓我明白
其實我正在改變世界

中文翻譯

2009 年初是我人生的一大轉捩點。克服種種困難之後,我進入了廣播界工作,在臺灣唯一的英語廣播電臺 ICRT 主持週末節目。我也是在這裡得到我的藝名 JR。一年之內,我從主持週末節目到主持平日午間節目。此時的我正享受著我人生中最快樂的時光之一。

2012 年,電臺給所有 DJ 一個新任務。在常態的節目之外,每個人要發想一個自己的深夜節目內容,一週一次,在凌晨 12 點播出。內容必須是獨特的、不同於白天節目。正當我的 DJ 夥伴們紛紛想出很棒的點子,像是獨立音樂、夜店混音、重金屬等等之時,我卻有點卡住了。「我可以為我的節目帶來什麼元素,是可以讓我跟其他 DJ 們有所區隔的呢?」我如此思索著。既然我是每週日上教會的電臺「乖寶寶」,所以最後我想到,我可以開一個有關正能量音樂的節目。我把它取名叫「午夜後的天光」,象徵即使在最深的黑夜之中,仍然帶著希望。

節目裡播的都是正能量音樂,還有啟發人心的談話,都是我很享受其中的內容。但即便如此,我還是感到懷疑:「我做的這些,真的對這世界有影響嗎?」我的深夜聽眾人數不到我白天節目的三分之一。加上我又看不到我的聽眾,我總有一種身處於隔離的房間,對著一支孤獨的麥克風說話的感覺。「我真的有觸碰到任何一個人的內心嗎?」我困惑著。

有一天,我收到了一個叫 Jenny 的女生來信。Jenny 剛考上大學,寫信告訴我,她高中時有多麼喜歡收聽「午夜後的天光」。每週二晚上,她會在熬夜念書準備考試的時候,打開廣播收聽節目。Jenny 告訴我,這個節目幫助她撐過了艱難的高中生活,也對她的人生產生重大的改變。她的信裡附了一個附件,那是她當年收聽我節目時所抄下的所有筆記照片。

一直到現在,我還是經常用這故事提醒自己,即便我做的事情再怎麼微小,我其實還是影響著人們。一點一滴、一個人一個人地累積、一顆內心一顆內心地改變,我們或許無法拯救世界,但我們絕對能改變它。

Vocabulary & Phrases
單字片語

※ 底線單字為「複習單字」，為之前出現過的字。

---

1. turning point │轉捩點，轉機

It's fair to say that the turning point in Emilia Clarke's career came when she starred as the Mother of Dragons in *Game of Thrones*.
如果要說艾蜜莉亞克拉克出演《權力遊戲》的龍母一角是她事業的轉捩點，這一點也不為過。

* **it's fair to say** │說……並不為過

---

2. against all/the odds │儘管困難重重；在極為不利的情況下

Against all odds, they managed to pull off a huge charity event for children in need.
即便困難重重，他們還是設法成功舉辦了一個大規模的兒童慈善活動。

---

3. blossom [ˋblɑsəm] (v.) │開花；成長，發展，興旺

Over the course of time, a search engine prototype named BackRub, which was designed by a pair of Ph.D. students at Stanford, blossomed into what we now know as Google.
經歷一段時間之後，一個由幾位史丹佛大學博士生所設計的原型搜尋引擎 BackRub 發展成現在眾所皆知的 Google。

* **in/over the course of time** │經過一段時間；最後

---

4. air [ɛr] (v.) │（透過廣播或電視）播送，播放

The classical music show airs every evening at 8 p.m.
該古典音樂節目每天晚上八點播放。

---

5. come up with │ 想出，提出（主意或計劃）

Jack came up with a brilliant idea on how to attract more traffic to the company website.
傑克想到了一個幫助公司網站吸引更多流量的超棒點子。

....

6. be strapped for │ 缺少

一般常以 strapped for cash 表達，指「手頭很緊，缺錢」。

Before Daniel got this new job, he was seriously strapped for cash.
丹尼爾在拿到這分新工作前，他真的沒錢了。

....

7. differentiate sb./sth. from sb./sth. │ 把……跟……區分開來

| Jenny: | I can barely differentiate this design from the other. | 珍妮：我幾乎分不出這個設計跟另一個有什麼差別。 |
| Gina: | I know. They're basically identical. | 吉娜：就是說啊，它們基本上是一模一樣的。 |

....

8. uplifting [ʌpˋlɪftɪŋ] (adj.) │ 令人振奮的，使人開心的

There's nothing like listening to some uplifting music while reading your favorite book in a comfy coffee shop.
坐在舒服的咖啡廳裡，一邊聽著振奮人心的音樂，一邊讀著自己最喜歡的書，再也沒有比這更棒的事了。

* comfy [ˋkʌmfɪ] (adj.) │ 舒服的，舒適的，等於 comfortable。

....

9. solitary [ˋsɑləˏtɛrɪ] (adj.) │ 獨自的，單獨的

The prisoner was put in solitary confinement.
該囚犯被單獨監禁。

....

10. lift one's spirits │ 使某人感到開心

(Gina is feeling down today.)	（吉娜今天感到心情沮喪。）
Tommy: Honey, what can I do to lift your spirits?	湯米：親愛的，我可以做什麼讓妳感到開心呢？
Gina: You can buy me a diamond ring. That'll do.	吉娜：你可以買顆鑽戒給我，這樣應該就行了。

11. have/make an impact on sb./sth. | 對……產生影響

The way parents interact with each other has a long-lasting impact on their children.

父母之間的互動方式會對孩子產生深遠的影響。

Now what I'd like to suggest is that you're not going to get only one car in your lifetime, but you're gonna get one body and one mind, and that's all you're gonna get. And that body and mind feels terrific now, but it has to last you a lifetime.

我想說的是，這輩子你不會只開一輛車，但你只會有一副身軀跟一顆內心，就只會有這麼多了。你可能覺得現在的身心狀態處在巔峰，但是這副身心必須要夠你使用一輩子。

——股神
Warren Buffett 巴菲特

The Biggest ˈA [1]

人生最大的資產

My life has always been filled with endless activities. In my **❶spare time**, I read tons of books, traveled a lot, and attended countless events. However, that was all before my [2]**hectic** YouTube career started, when I still had the luxury of "**❶me time**." Nowadays I feel like **❷a slave to the clock**. No matter how hard I work to get **❸ahead of schedule**, there always seems to be another video to make or another thing to [3]**cross off** of my to-do list.

Luckily, I've long had the habit of writing my experiences down in a notebook. I can always take a step back in time and relive the things I experienced back when I had more free time. This serves as a great source of inspiration for my video-making, or in this case, book-writing.

Several years ago, I attended a speech titled The Wisdom of Life, which was [4]**delivered** by an old preacher to a crowd of young people. Halfway through the speech, he [5]**raised a question**, asking everybody present, "What do you think the biggest asset in life is?" People started raising their hands and giving their answers. "Family," said one. "Health," said another. "Time," said a third. "My credit card," someone in the crowd yelled out, and the audience [6]**burst into laughter**.

The preacher paused for a second before speaking up again. "I think all your answers make sense, but I think my answer is quite good too," he said. "The biggest asset in life is your character, your personality. And the reason why is because that's the only thing that'll follow you all the way through this life, 24 hours a day, 365 days a year. Everything else eventually disappears in the course of time, but your character will be

sset in Life

051

#16

with you till the day you die."

To this day, I barely remember the rest of the speech. But that question got ⁷**embedded** in my head. Isn't it so true that your character, good or bad, is the one thing that'll ⁸**stick with** you forever? No matter what other people think of your personality, whether good or bad, you are always going to be the first and last person who has to live with it. What else could be more important than that?

※ 底線單字為「複習單字」，為之前出現過的字。

❸ **ahead of schedule**

跑在行程前面，顧名思義就是「進度超前」。相反地，「進度落後」就是 **behind schedule**，另外也可以用 **on track**，代表「事情如預期順利進行中」。

我的大學教授曾說過：「如果你的一生時間只夠你讀一百本書，那這一百本書最好都是精挑細選過的。」這句話也可以套用在所有的事物上。如果我們能投資的時間和精力有限，那麼究竟有哪些東西是值得我們去學習和追求的呢？

JR的話

The Biggest Asset in Life

人生最大的資產

中文翻譯

我的生活總是圍繞著無止盡的活動，過去我經常在閒暇之餘閱讀、旅遊、參加許多活動。不過，那都是在我開始從事忙碌的 YouTube 事業之前的事了，在我還能享受「個人時間」這奢侈品的時候。如今我總是被時間追著跑，不管我有多努力想超前工作，似乎總是有另一部影片要做、有另一件事要從待辦事項上劃掉。

幸好，我從以前就有做筆記記下所見所聞的習慣。我總是能回到過去，複習那些我過去還有很多閒暇時間時所經歷過的事。這對我做影片來說，是一個很棒的靈感池，現在，則成了我寫書的靈感來源。

幾年前我參加了一位老牧師主講的演講，主題是「人生的智慧」，臺下是一群年輕人。演講到一半，他提出一個問題，他問現場所有人說：「你們認為人生最大的資產是什麼？」人們開始舉手回答。「家庭」「健康」「時間」「我的信用卡」，人群中有人喊出了這個答案，頓時全場哄堂大笑。

這位牧師停頓了一會兒後，又重新開口。「我覺得你們的答案都很有道理，但我覺得我的答案也挺好的。」他說，「人生中最大的資產是你的品格，你的個性。理由是，它是唯一一會跟著你一輩子的事物，一天二十四小時，一年三百六十五天，其他事物終究都會隨著時間消逝，但你的品格會黏著你，直到你離開人世的那一天。」

直到今天，我幾乎忘了其他的演講內容，但是那道問題深深地嵌入了我的腦海中。這豈不是再有道理不過了嗎？你的人格，無論是好是壞，是唯一一會跟著你一輩子的事物，不是嗎？不管別人怎麼評價你的個性，無論是好或壞，你總是會第一個、也會是最後一個需要跟它相處的人，還有什麼比這更重要呢？

Vocabulary & Phrases
單字片語

052

※ 底線單字為「複習單字」，為之前出現過的字。

---

1. asset [ˋæsɛt] (n.) | 資產，財產

The CEO of the company has assets of over seven million dollars, but most of them are under his wife's name.
公司執行長擁有的資產超過七百萬美金，但大部分都在他太太的名下。

* **under one's name** | 在法律上隸屬於某人

---

2. hectic [ˋhɛktɪk] (adj.) | 繁忙的，忙碌的

We have a hectic schedule tomorrow, so please make sure you arrive at 8 a.m. sharp.
我們明天行程很繁忙，請務必明天早上八點準時抵達。

* **sharp** [ʃɑrp] (adv.) | （時間）準時地

---

3. cross off | 劃掉，刪去

(Tommy and Gina are grocery shopping.)
Tommy: Hey, I got the veggies.
Gina: Thanks, honey. Remember to cross it off the grocery list.

（湯米和吉娜正在購買食物與日用品。）
湯米：嘿，蔬菜我拿了喔。
吉娜：謝謝你，親愛的，記得把它從購物清單上劃掉。

* **grocery** [ˋgrosərɪ] (n.) | 中文沒有完全對應的詞，指的是「（在超市買的）食物和日常生活用品」，常用複數 groceries。
* **veggie** [ˋvɛdʒɪ] (n.) | （美式英文）蔬菜，等同 vegetable。

4. deliver [dɪ`lɪvɚ] (v.) | 發表（演講）；寄送

deliver 用法也很廣泛，在本文中是指「發表演講」，除此之外也有「遞送貨物」的意思。

Who delivered the speech at your graduation ceremony?
你畢業典禮上是誰發表演說的？

....

5. raise/pose a question | 提出問題

跟 ask a question 稍有不同，ask a question 是詢問需要答案的問題，
而 raise/pose a question 則是提出值得深入思考的問題，好讓人意識到某議題。

此外，raise 也可以用來「舉起、引發」其他東西，如 raise your hand「舉手」，raise doubt「引起疑惑」，raise problems「引起問題」等。也有 raise money「募款」的用法，是用法相當廣泛的字。

The preacher posed a question about the meaning of life.
牧師提出了一個關於人生意義的問題。

....

6. burst into laughter/tears | 突然大笑或爆哭

The audience always burst into laughter when Kevin Hart starts telling jokes.
每當凱文哈特開始講笑話，全場觀眾就會哄堂大笑。

* **Kevin Hart** | 美國知名的喜劇諧星及電影明星。

....

7. embed [ɪm`bɛd] (v.) | 嵌入

Many aspects of culture are embedded in a country's language.
一個文化的許多方面都深植在該國的語言當中。

* **aspect** [`æspɛkt] (n.) | 方面；觀點

....

8. stick with sb./sth. | 堅持做某事；繼續相信某決定或信念

stick 是「黏住」的意思，stick with sb./sth. 是「緊緊跟著」之意，
另外也有「繼續使用或做某事；繼續相信某個決定或信念」的意思。

Some memories stick with you for a lifetime.
有些回憶會一輩子跟著你。

I don't like surprises, so let's stick with the original plan.
我不喜歡驚喜，我們按照原定計畫走。

I've failed over and over again in my life. And that is why I succeed.

我這一生總是一而再、再而三地失敗。然而,這正是我會成功的原因。

—— 籃球大帝
Michael Jordan 麥可喬丹

The Boxer
人生像一場拳擊賽

❶ boxing match

拳擊賽。球類比賽有的用 game，有的用 match 稱呼，究竟怎麼區分？事實上沒有明確的原則，不過，許多源自英格蘭的比賽會使用 match，如 tennis match「網球賽」，golf match「高爾夫球賽」，cricket match「板球賽」。而源自美國的比賽多用 game，如 baseball game「棒球賽」，basketball game「籃球賽」，football game「美式足球賽」。但這並非絕對，像是源自美國的排球賽是 volleyball match，而足球更是英美各自表態，美國稱 soccer game，英國叫 football match。而某些球類，譬如網球，一場比賽又包含 set「盤」和 game「局」。

❷ be on the ropes

被逼到擂臺圍繩（ropes）的拳手是處於下風的，因此 be on the ropes 既是實際指拳賽中被逼到圍繩上，也有「處境很糟，瀕臨失敗」的意思。

My friend Joanne once told me a story that [1]**made a difference** in her life. Somehow, it got [2]**stuck in my head** too.

Ever since graduating from high school, Joanne has been in close touch with one of her teachers—a wartime [3]**veteran** who went through many [4]**ups and downs** in a [5]**turbulent** era. You can tell how much Joanne respects him.

One day she went to visit her old friend. She'd just suffered a major [6]**setback** and was feeling pretty beaten down. They talked about it over dinner with the TV on in the background. After a while, the old man asked Joanne to take a look at what was on TV. It was a live broadcast of a ❶**boxing match**.

Now my friend is no fan of any violent sport. And she was quick to reveal it with the look on her face. But the old man asked her to [7]**bear with** him for a moment.

"You see that guy in the blue shorts? I bet he's gonna lose," he said.

The boxer in blue shorts ❷**was on the ropes** and [8]**taking a beating**. His legs were [9]**wobbling**, his left eye was [10]**swollen**, and his nose was bleeding.

"This is so cruel," Joanne replied with a [11]**frown**. "[12]**With all due respect**, why would anyone be interested in boxing [13]**in the first place**?"

"Well, you can actually learn a lot from it. You see, a boxer hardly ever gets knocked down in one ¹⁴**blow**. In fact, you'd be surprised how many hits a person can take. Now look at the boxer with the <u>upper hand</u>…"

The guy was throwing wild punches like a madman. Each ¹⁵**swing** brought him one step closer to victory. But he was tired and <u>injured</u> too. Then the old man <u>delivered</u> his "❸**punchline**."

"You see, nobody wins without taking some heavy hits too. Once you step in the <u>ring</u>, win or lose, no one escapes ¹⁶**without a scratch**. But what ¹⁷**separates** the winners **from** the losers is the ¹⁸**determination** it takes to stay standing till the final bell rings. And young woman, it's the same with life."

Joanne smiled. Her old teacher always had an ¹⁹**exceptional** way of ²⁰**getting** his message **across**.

※ 底線單字為「複習單字」，為之前出現過的字。

❸ punchline

梗，妙語。punchline 意思是「（故事最後點題或點出笑料的）一句妙語，畫龍點睛的結尾句」，類似中文的「梗」，也就是「故事亮點、笑梗」。我在本篇文章用 punchline 跟 punch 玩雙關語，取 punch 原本就是「出拳」的意思，跟 punchline「梗」玩雙關語。

JR YouTube
影片 #15

我的經驗告訴我，實力和技術很重要，但是精神和態度，更是左右成敗的關鍵。

JR的話

The Boxer

人生像一場拳擊賽

我的好友瓊安曾告訴我一個改變她生命的故事。不知怎麼地,這故事就深深烙印在我腦海中了。

瓊安從中學畢業之後,就和一名老師保持著密切聯繫。他是戰爭時期的退伍軍人,經歷了紛擾不安的戰爭歲月。看得出來,瓊安非常尊敬他。

有天,她去探望這位老友。她才剛經歷了重大的挫折,感到相當挫敗。在晚餐時間,他們開著電視,聊到了這件事。過了一會兒,老先生叫瓊安看一下電視。電視上正在轉播一場拳擊賽。

我的朋友可一點都不喜歡任何有暴力的運動。她的感受馬上寫在臉上,但是老先生要她稍微擔待一下,陪他一起看。

他說:「妳看到那個穿藍色短褲的傢伙嗎?我賭他會輸。」

穿著藍色短褲的拳擊手被逼到繩邊,被打得毫無招架之力。他的雙腳搖晃得很厲害,左眼腫了起來,鼻子還流著血。

瓊安蹙著眉說:「這好殘忍,恕我直言,到底為什麼會有人對拳擊感興趣?」

「這個嘛,其實妳可以從中學到很多。妳看,拳擊手很少有一拳就被擊倒的。事實上,如果妳知道一個人可以承受多少打擊,妳會感到很驚訝。現在,妳看那個佔上風的拳手⋯⋯」

那傢伙發瘋似地猛烈揮拳。每一次出拳,他就離勝利更近一步。但是,他其實也既疲憊又全身是傷。接著,老先生說出了他的「梗」。

「妳看,沒有人可以在不挨拳的情況下獲勝。你一旦上場,非輸即贏,沒人能毫髮無傷。但是,區分出贏家與輸者的關鍵在於,你是否有一直站在場上直到最後鈴響的決心。人生也是如此啊,年輕女士。」

瓊安露出了笑容。她的年邁老師總是有他一套傳達道理的方法。

Vocabulary & Phrases
單字片語

054

※ 底線單字為「複習單字」，為之前出現過的字。

---

1. make a difference │ 產生（正面的）影響；讓社會、世界更美好

Exercising just 30 minutes a day can make a big difference in your health.
每天運動三十分鐘會為你的健康帶來顯著的改變。

---

2. stick in one's mind/head │ 難以忘懷

The image of the fatal car accident was so shocking it stuck in her mind for a long time.
死亡車禍的畫面太過於震驚，以至於她久久無法忘記。

---

3. veteran [ˈvɛtərən] (n.) │ 老兵，退伍軍人；經驗豐富的老手

---

4. ups and downs │（人生經歷的）浮沉，起起伏伏

I've had my fair share of ups and downs in life, but I've always felt content with what I have.
我經歷過許多人生的波折起伏，但我始終對於我所擁有的感到知足。

* **have one's (fair) share of sth.** │ 經歷太多（問題或壞事）

* **content** [kənˈtɛnt] (adj.) │ 在這裡當形容詞，指「感到滿足的」

---

5. turbulent [ˈtɜbjələnt] (adj.) │ 騷亂的，動盪不安的

2020 has been a turbulent year due to the novel coronavirus outbreak.
新型冠狀型病毒的爆發，讓 2020 年成為動盪不安的一年。

6. setback [ˋsɛt.bæk] (n.) │ 挫折，失敗，阻礙

若要當動詞用，可以說 set sb./sth. back「使某人某事感到挫折」。

Jack:	There's been a minor setback in the renovation plans. But don't worry, we're gonna deal with it <u>in no time</u>.
Tommy:	Jack, you're the only one who's <u>losing his head over it</u>.

傑克：我們翻新計劃上遇到了點小挫敗，但是不要擔心，我們會快速搞定的。

湯米：傑克，只有你一個人在那邊慌張。

......

7. bear with │ 容忍，擔待

Tommy:	Bob, you know you tell bad jokes, don't you?
Bob:	I know, I know, but bear with me for just one more. This is really a good one!

湯米：鮑伯，你應該知道你講的笑話都很冷吧？

鮑伯：我知道，我知道，但是你再擔待一下，讓我講最後一個，這個包準好笑！

......

8. take a beating │ 挨打；承受打擊

The global economy took a serious beating during the 2008 financial crisis.
全球經濟在 2008 年金融危機期間受到嚴重打擊。

......

9. wobble [ˋwɑbl] (v.) │ 搖晃；不穩定

George was so nervous about his speech that his knees started to wobble.
喬治想到演講的事就緊張到膝蓋發抖。

......

10. swell [swɛl] (v.) │ 腫起，腫脹

The sprain in my ankle caused it to swell badly.
我的腳踝扭傷，造成它腫得很厲害。

......

11. frown [fraʊn] (v.)/(n.) │ 皺眉

frown 當動詞時也有「不贊成」的意思，常用以下片語表達：frown on/upon sth.「不贊同某事」。

12. with all due respect │（禮貌地表達異議）恕我直言

With all due respect, our company frowns on this kind of behavior.
恕我直言，我們公司不贊同這樣的行為。

13. in the first place │原本，最初

How was I supposed to know? You should've told me in the first place.
我怎麼會知道？你應該一開始就告訴我。

14. blow [blo] (n.) │（用拳頭或重物）重擊

The boxer received a blow to the head.
該拳擊手頭部遭受重重一擊。

15. swing [swiŋ] (n.)/(v.) │揮動拳頭或器物

swing 如果用在網球上，就是「揮拍」的意思。

The drunk took a swing at me but missed.
該名醉漢朝我揮拳，但是揮空。

16. without a scratch │毫髮無傷

Jack's ride flipped on the underline freeway while going 90 miles per hour. Miraculously, he escaped without a scratch.
傑克開著愛車以時速九十英里在高速公路上翻車了，奇蹟似地，他毫髮無傷。

* ride [raɪd] (n.) │（口語）個人車輛

17. separate from │將……分開；辨別……

Nobody can separate Tommy from Gina. He's stuck to her like glue.
沒有人可以把湯米跟吉娜分開，他就像膠水一樣黏在她身上。

* stick to sb. like glue │緊黏某人

18. determination [dɪˌtɜmə`neʃən] (n.) | 決心

Her determination to make a difference in the world is truly admirable.
她想要改變世界的決心讓人真心感到欽佩。

....

19. exceptional [ɪk`sɛpʃənəl] (adj.) | 非凡的；優異的，卓越的

The way Lionel Messi controls the ball on the <u>pitch</u> is exceptional!
梅西在足球場上控球的表現簡直是不可思議！

....

20. get sth. across | 理解某事；把某事說清楚

Tommy sometimes has trouble getting his meaning across in Chinese.
湯米有時很難用中文清楚傳達意思。

More Expressions
Personality 個性相關單字片語

born optimist | 天性樂觀的人

good egg | 好人

culture vulture | 熱衷文化藝術的人

bag egg | 壞蛋

好蛋就是形容「好人」。相反地，壞人就是 bad egg。

dark horse | 黑馬

eager beaver | 拼命工作的人

河狸是一種很勤勞的動物，所以熱切的 (eager) 河狸 (beaver) 就是形容「工作非常賣力、甚至過頭的人」。

go-getter (n.) | 專心致志的人

形容設定好目標就會達成的人。

jack-of-all-trades (n.) | 廣而不精的人

形容一個人什麼都懂，但是也可以用來貶人，所謂的「樣樣通，樣樣鬆」就是英文的 jack-of-all-trades, master of none.

early bird | 早起的人

我想不必多解釋，誠如諺語 The early bird gets the worm. (早起的鳥兒有蟲吃。)

family man / woman | 顧家的人

man of his word / woman of her word | 信守承諾的人

smart cookie | 聰明、機靈的人

fast-talker (n.) | 花言巧語的人

不是形容人說話很快喔！而是形容一個人能言善道，很會說服別人去做自己意圖的事，帶有貶意。

cheapskate (n.) | 吝嗇鬼，小氣鬼

goody-goody (n.) | 乖寶寶，乖乖牌

喜歡在師長、長官面前賣乖的人。

busybody (n.) | 愛多管閒事的人

另一個相似的詞是 meddler。

gold digger | 拜金女

know-it-all (n.) | **自以為無所不知的人**

總是表現得好像什麼都懂的人，帶有貶意，類似的詞還有 wise guy、smart aleck 等。

black sheep | **害群之馬**

armchair critic | **出一張嘴的人**

坐在扶手椅 (armchair) 上的評論家 (critic)，就是指那些沒有相關經驗卻又愛發表評論、批判的人。

loose cannon | **我行我素的人**

大砲 (cannon) 如果沒有固定好 (loose) 就發射，砲座可會被反作用力彈飛，所以這是形容「不受控、我行我素的人」。

party pooper | **掃興的人**

在派對上大便的人 (pooper)，形容一個人很掃興。

big mouth | **大嘴巴**

可以說 sb. is a big mouth 或者 sb. has a big mouth。

couch potato | **沙發馬鈴薯**

就是「成天到晚坐在沙發上看電視的懶惰鬼」。

teacher's pet | **老師最喜歡的學生**

老師的寵物 (pet) 是什麼？就是指「最受老師寵愛的學生」。老師眼裡的好學生，通常是同學們眼中的討厭鬼，所以這個詞常帶有貶意。

如何正面形容一個人？

a good laugh | **風趣幽默的**

形容一個人很有趣，在其身邊總是充滿歡笑。

bright / sharp (adj.) | **聰穎機伶的**

明亮和銳利，這兩個都是形容人很聰明，後者 (sharp) 除了聰明，也有精明的意思。

down to earth | **腳踏實地的**

easy-going (adj.) | **隨和的，好相處的**

open-minded (adj.) | **開明的，心胸開闊的**

相反的意思就是 narrow-minded。

straightforward (adj.) | **直率的**

如何負面形容一個人？

a pain in the neck | **討人厭的**

脖子 (neck) 上總有一股疼痛 (pain)，指一個人非常令人討厭。

pig-headed (adj.) | **固執的**

不是豬頭啦！是形容一個人很固執 (stubborn)。

be full of oneself | **自以為了不起**

big-headed (adj.) | **有大頭症的**

沒錯，按照其字面翻譯就是「大頭症」啦！形容一個人自以為自己很重要、很聰明。

tight (adj.) | **吝嗇小氣的**

tight 一字可以形容很多事情，tight-lipped 是「口風很緊」，on a tight budget 是「預算很緊」，如果說一個人很 tight，則有「(口語) 吝嗇，很摳」的意思。

have a screw loose | **有點無厘頭，怪怪的**

身上有處螺絲 (screw) 鬆了 (loose)，代表一個人「行為舉止怪異，神經有點不正常」。

have a short fuse | **脾氣急躁、易怒的**

炸藥引信 (fuse) 很短 (short)，表示很容易爆炸，形容一個人「容易生氣、易怒的」。

nuts (adj.) | **瘋狂的**

瘋了的意思，跟 crazy 相同。也可以形容一件事超厲害的：That's nuts!（太狂了！）

thick as a plank | **很笨，笨極了**

**not the brightest crayon in the box /
not the sharpest tool in the shed
不太聰明的**

在本篇有提到 bright 和 sharp 可以形容人很聰明，也可以用在這裡的兩個詞。首先，不是盒子裡最鮮豔 (bright) 的蠟筆，就是指某人「不是很聰明」；不是庫房 (shed) 裡最銳利 (sharp) 的工具，也是指同樣意思。

**have one's head in the clouds
不切實際的；天馬行空的**

活在雲端裡，形容想法不切實際。

正能量
座右銘
MOTTO

Just as a picture is taken exactly in the way you take it with a camera, whatever you see, hear, and think are stored exactly as is in the brain.

如同用相機照相，事物就會如實被照下來一般，你所看、所聽、所想的，也會如實存放在腦中。

——出自 JR 的筆記本

The ¹Choir B

詩班男孩

❶ be flooded with sth.

flood 是「淹水」的名詞和動詞，be flooded with sth. 指的是「充斥著……」。

....

❷ pulpit

講道壇。就是教堂中神父站在最前面講道的地方。

....

❸ live in a cave

與現實世界脫節。也可以作 live under a rock，字面意思是住在山洞裡，因此衍伸為「跟現實環境、思想、活動脫節」，常用在玩笑話或戲謔的對話中。

This is based on a true story I heard that really made me think about how people can rule their own minds.

One sunny Sunday morning, a young mother went to the front of the church after service to ask the preacher a question that was ²**lingering** in her mind. These days, the media and the Internet ❶**are flooded with** all sorts of information, and not all of it is positive and healthy. So ³**on behalf of** her children, the worried mother asked, "Pastor, how can we protect our children in a world full of sex, drugs, ⁴**slander** and ⁵**violence**? It's like the minute I turn away, they could ⁶**be exposed to** any of that."

It was a question that every parent had thought about before, so a small crowd of people gathered around the ❷**pulpit** to hear what the preacher had to say. The preacher paused and ⁷**contemplated** for a short while, and then turned to a teenager in the choir and asked him to come over.

"Jonathan, would you please be kind enough to sing a ⁸**hymn**?" the preacher asked politely.

This was totally unexpected, and everyone stuck around to see what would happen next. The boy sang a hymn, and when he finished, the crowd ⁹**applauded** loudly. Then the preacher looked at the young mother again and said, "Is there any possible way for you to ¹⁰**isolate** your children from the awful things you've mentioned?"

"Pastor, aside from ❸**living in a cave**, I don't think there's anything we can do to stop our children from coming into contact with that kind of information," the mother replied.

"Right. So we can't isolate ourselves from the world. And we can't change it with a snap of our fingers, though sometimes I wish we could.

So here's what I think."

The preacher turned to the choir boy and asked, "Jonathan, what was on your mind while you were singing just then?"

"Why, of course I was thinking about God, Pastor. The lyrics are all about God."

"Did you have any [11]**malicious** thoughts?" the preacher asked.

"Of course not, Pastor," the boy replied.

The preacher turned back to the crowd with a smile and said, "This young lad here says God was all he thought about while he was singing. Do you believe him?"

The crowd laughed and responded with a [12]**unanimous** "Yes."

"I believe him, too. Now the way I see it, we don't always have control over the environment, our surroundings, but there is one thing we can control," said the preacher, pointing to his head. "The mind. The mind is like a video camera—it records everything it [13]**crosses paths with**, both good and bad. What we can do is—feed the mind with good things. Keep the mind busy processing the good, and thereby leaving no space for the bad. You see, we might not be able to [14]**eradicate** evil, but we can definitely [15]**occupy** our minds with good."

影片是重新編寫的，所以內容跟這裡稍有不同喔！

JR YouTube
影片 #16

※ 底線單字為「複習單字」，為之前出現過的字。

JR的話

回想我自己過去到現在，我發現，自己的個性往好的方面改變了很多。我認為，這跟我長期接觸正向的思維與事物有關。人的內心像一塊海綿，會強力地吸收所接觸到的任何事物或經驗，所以我們應該要負起責任，常常給它「好的事物」。

The Choir Boy
詩班男孩

這篇文章是根據我聽到的真實故事，讓我認真思考，人們是如何能治理自己的內心。

某個陽光普照的夏日早晨，一位年輕媽媽做完禮拜後，來到教會前面，問了牧師一個縈繞她內心許久的問題。這年頭媒體跟網路上充斥著各種資訊，不是所有的都很正面、健康。所以這位憂心的母親為了自己的孩子向牧師發問：「牧師啊，我們該如何保護自己的孩子，遠離充滿色情、毒品、毀謗與暴力的世界？好像只要我一分神，他們就會暴露在這些事物之中。」

這是每位當父母的都曾想過的問題，所以在講壇前，慢慢地，一群人聚集了過來，大家都想聽牧師怎麼說。牧師停頓沉思了一會兒，接著轉向詩班中的一名少年，請他過來。

「強納森，可以請你小唱一段詩歌嗎？」牧師有禮地拜託。

這個請求出乎大家意料，每個人面面相覷，想看接下來會發生什麼事。男孩唱了一段詩歌，當他唱完，群眾大聲地拍手。接著牧師看向那名年輕媽媽說：「有沒有任何方法，可以把你的孩子們跟剛剛你提到的這些糟糕的事物隔離呢？」

「牧師，除非我們完全與世隔絕，否則無法阻止孩子不接觸那些資訊。」那位母親回答。

「那就是了。我們並不能將自己完全與世界隔絕開來。我們也不能彈個手指就改變世界，雖然有時候我希望自己可以。所以，以下是我的想法。」

牧師轉向那名詩班的男孩，問他：「強納森，你剛剛唱歌的時候在想什麼？」

「這，我想的當然是神啊，牧師。歌詞寫的都是有關神。」

「你有產生任何邪惡的想法嗎？」牧師繼續問。

「當然沒有，牧師。」男孩回答。

牧師轉向群眾，微笑地說：「這名年輕小伙子說他唱歌的時候，心裡想的都是神。你們相信嗎？」

大家都笑了，異口同聲地回答「相信」。

「我也相信他。我是這麼看的，我們不能控制環境與生活周遭，但有一件事情是我們能控制的。」牧師一邊說，一邊指向自己的腦袋，「我們的心。心就像攝影機──它記錄下所見的每件事情，無論好壞。而我們可以做的，就是用好的事物餵養我們的內心。讓我們的心忙著接收好的事物，如此就沒有空間接收不好的事。你看，我們或許無法消除惡，但我們絕對可以用美好的事物填滿我們的內心。」

Vocabulary & Phrases
單字片語

※ 底線單字為「複習單字」，為之前出現過的字。

1. choir [kwaɪr] *(n.)* │ 唱詩班；合唱團

2. lingering [ˈlɪŋgəɪŋ] *(adj.)* │ 持續的，揮之不去的

Jack has had lingering nightmares ever since he got into that car accident.
傑克自從出了車禍之後，就不停做著這些揮之不去的惡夢。

3. on behalf of │ 代表；為了……的利益

The singer is raising money for charity on behalf of the earthquake victims' families.
那名歌手為了地震受難者家屬做慈善募款。

4. slander [ˈslændə] *(n.)/(v.)* │ 誹謗，詆毀

The newspaper was sued for slander after publishing the fake story about the star.
該報社因為報導那位明星的假消息而被告毀謗。

5. violence [ˈvaɪələns] *(n.)* │ 暴力

People should learn how to settle their arguments without resorting to violence.
人們應該要學習在不使用暴力的情況下解決紛爭。

* resort to │ 訴諸、憑藉（某種手段）

6. be exposed to | 暴露於，接觸到

Soldiers were exposed to sniper fire during the battle for the city.
在奪城戰役中，士兵暴露在狙擊手的火力之中。

7. contemplate [ˋkɑntɛmpˏlet] (v.) | 思量，仔細考慮

Gina is contemplating going <u>abroad</u> for advanced study.
吉娜正在審慎考慮是否要出國深造。

8. hymn [hɪm] (n.) | 讚美詩歌，聖歌

9. applaud [əˋplɔd] (v.) | 鼓掌，喝采

The <u>audience</u> applauded for two minutes straight after Jenny's performance.
珍妮表演結束之後，觀眾鼓掌了兩分鐘之久。

10. isolate [ˋaɪsəˏlet] (v.) | 孤立，隔離

People who test positive for the virus must be isolated from the general public.
驗出病毒陽性的人，必須跟社會大眾隔離。

* general public | 一般民眾，社會大眾

11. malicious [məˋlɪʃəs] (adj.) | 惡意的，蓄意傷人的

The article was full of malicious slander meant to damage the company's reputation.
那篇文章充滿惡意的誹謗，用意就是要重傷公司聲譽。

* reputation [ˏrɛpjəˋteʃən] (n.) | 名譽，名聲

12. unanimous [juˋnænəməs] (adj.) | 全體一致的，一致同意的，無異議的

The vote to take a company trip to Hawaii was unanimous.
公司旅遊去夏威夷的投票結果全體一致通過。

13. cross paths with sb./sth. | 碰上某人某事

I know he's giving you trouble, but look on the bright side—you'll never have to cross paths with him after tomorrow.

我知道他在找你麻煩，但是往好的方面想，明天過後你就再也不用看到他了。

* **look on the bright side** | 看到好的一面，往好的方面想

....

14. eradicate [ɪˈrædɪˌket] (v.) | 根除，消滅，杜絕

Unfortunately, we are still far from achieving the goals of eradicating global poverty.

不幸的是，我們距離消除全球貧窮的目標還有一大段距離。

....

15. occupy [ˈɑkjəˌpaɪ] (v.) | 佔領，佔據

Writing this book has occupied most of my time over the past year.

寫這本書佔據了我過去一年大部分的時間。

正能量
座右銘
MOTTO

For the past 33 years, I have looked in the mirror every morning and asked myself: 'If today were the last day of my life, would I want to do what I am about to do today?' And whenever the answer has been 'No' for too many days in a row, I know I need to change something.

過去三十三年來，我每天早上都會看著鏡子問自己：「如果今天是我生命的最後一天，我還會想做我今天要做的事嗎？」每當有一連好幾天答案都是「不」的時候，我就知道我必須要做出改變。

―― 蘋果創辦人
Steve Jobs 賈伯斯

I Was the Shies

我曾是班上最害羞的孩子

❶ introvert

introvert 是「性格內向者」，形容詞是 introverted「內向的」，introversion 則是名詞「內向」。反義詞則是 extrovert「性格外向者」，extroverted「外向的」和 extroversion。

....

❷ Yeah, right!

非常口語的英文，故意說反話來表達自己不相信對方，也就是中文的「最好是啦！」

....

❸ Get out of here!

雖然在某些場合是指「滾出去！」的意思，但在這裡是表達不相信對方所說，通常在熟人之間才會講，類似中文的「少來了！」或「真的假的！」。跟 Yeah, right! 稍有不同的是 Get out of here! 帶有驚訝口氣，而 Yeah, right! 則有諷刺意味。

Whenever I say that I'm an ❶**introvert**, the reaction I usually get is, ❷**"Yeah, right!"** or ❸**"Get out of here!"** Nobody really takes me seriously. But I'm 100% serious. I can understand why people don't believe me. They see me making YouTube videos, giving speeches and hosting radio shows—all things that seem to require an outgoing personality. But the truth is, I had to intentionally train myself in order to stand in the limelight without [1]**shaking like a leaf**.

While there is a [2]**subtle** difference between being shy and being ❶**introverted**, I consider myself both. As a kid, I would always hide whenever we had visitors at our house. On the first day of fourth grade, which was also the first day I attended school in Taiwan, the teacher asked me to go to the front of the class and introduce myself. I'll never forget how I [3]**leaned** against the chalkboard [4]**shivering** like a frightened animal! To be honest, I hated myself like that. And my parents weren't too happy about it either. "Why can't I just be confident and outgoing like the cool kids?" I often thought to myself.

I started thinking about how I could change, and soon found my chance for a brand new start—junior high school. So on the first day of junior high, I anxiously picked a seat in the middle of the classroom. Then in my head I [5]**commanded** myself, "Talk to the classmate sitting on your right." It took a lot of ❹**guts** for a kid like me to do so, but I did it. And it wasn't as frightening as I thought it would be. So then I told myself, "Now talk to the kid on your left." And I did that too. For the rest of the day, I kept talking to different kids in my class. It got easier and easier, and I felt more and more comfortable doing so. By the end of the day, I was [6]**elected** class secretary, which was a first for me.

Kid in Class

057

#19

I got better and better at handling my <u>anxiety</u> around people. Don't <u>get me wrong</u> though. Things didn't ⁷**happen overnight**. I remember running off stage in the middle of a speech contest once. And I was always afraid to ⁸**strike up conversations with** strangers, especially girls. I had to ⁹**force** myself to keep ¹⁰**pushing my boundaries**, and I'm still ¹¹**far from** that ideal confident, ¹²**charismatic** <u>figure</u> I wish I could be. But that's okay! Nothing will change the fact that I'm an introverted person. I still ❺**get butterflies in my stomach** every time I'm about to hit the stage. But I've changed the way I deal with it. And just look at how far I've come. If I can do it, then so can you.

※ 底線單字為「複習單字」，為之前出現過的字。

❹ **guts**

gut(s) 有「腸道」的意思，不過這裡的 guts 是「勇氣，膽量，意志」，所以說 **You have guts!** 就是「你有種！」**You don't have the guts.**（你沒那個膽。）而 gut 又可以當作「直覺，本能」，譬如：**I have a gut feeling...**（我有直覺……），**My gut tells me...**（我的直覺告訴我……）。

❺ **have/get butterflies in one's stomach**

可以想像蝴蝶（**butterfly**）在肚子（**stomach**）裡亂飛嗎？意思就是「對某事感到非常緊張不安」。

別看我做影片、主持廣播節目、四處演講，好像很大方健談，但其實我是一個內向的人（內向、外向，沒有哪一個比較好），連我最要好的朋友們都不相信我本性很內向。重點不在於自己生來擁有什麼樣的特質，而是你如何在這些特質的基礎之上，塑造、造就並改變自己。我以我親身的經驗，跟你分享這一點。

JR 的話

I Was the Shiest Kid in Class

我曾是班上最害羞的孩子

中文翻譯

每當我說我是個內向的人的時候，我得到的回應往往是：「最好是啦！」或是「你少來了！」沒人真的把我的話當一回事。不過我是百分之一萬認真的。我可以理解為什麼大家不相信。他們看我拍 YouTube 影片，到處演講，還主持廣播節目 —— 都是些看似需要外向個性的事情。不過事實是，我過去是刻意訓練自己，才有辦法站在鎂光燈下而不瑟瑟發抖。

內向跟害羞其實有些微不同，不過我認為我兩個都是。我小的時候，家裡只要有客人來，我總是跑去躲起來。我升四年級的第一天，也是我第一次上臺灣的學校，老師要我上臺自我介紹。我永遠忘不了，我靠在黑板邊、像個被嚇壞的動物一樣發抖！坦白說，我超討厭那樣的自己。而我爸媽也不太喜歡我這樣。「為什麼我不能像學校裡那些受歡迎的同學那樣自信外向呢？」我常常問自己。

我開始思考，我該如何改變自己。很快地，我找到一個全新開始的機會 ——國中。在上國中的第一天，我焦慮地在教室裡挑了一個位子坐下來。接著，我在腦海裡命令自己：「跟坐在你右邊的同學講話。」要我這樣的孩子做出這種事情，是需要很大的勇氣，但是我做了。而我發現，這並沒有想像中可怕。所以我接著跟自己說：「現在跟你左邊的同學講話。」而我也做了。當天，我持續跟班上不同的同學講話。一次比一次簡單，而我也感到越來越自在。在放學之前，我被選為班上的學藝股長，這還是我第一次當班級幹部。

我越來越會處理跟他人互動時產生的焦慮。不過可別誤會了，這改變並非一夜之間發生。我記得有次我參加演講比賽，講到一半還從講臺上跑了下來。我總是害怕跟陌生人談話，尤其是女生。我必須持續挑戰我自己的極限，而我距離理想中的那個自信、有魅力的形象還差得遠。不過沒關係！我骨子裡是個內向的人是不會改變的事實。我每次要上臺前還是會緊張不安。但是，我已經改變處理自己焦慮的方式。看看我至今所做出的改變，我可以的話，你一定也可以。

Vocabulary & Phrases
單字片語

058

※ 底線單字為「複習單字」，為之前出現過的字。

---

1. shake like a leaf ｜ 緊張害怕到發抖

像風吹抖動的葉子一般，意思是「因為害怕或緊張而緊張得發抖」。

Tommy: I can picture myself shaking like a leaf on our wedding day.

Gina: You're not having second thoughts about getting married, are you?

湯米：我可以想像，我在結婚那天緊張發抖的樣子。

吉娜：你該不會對結婚這件事猶豫了吧？

---

2. subtle [ˈsʌtl] (adj.) ｜ 隱約的，不易察覺的

If you look carefully, you can still spot a few subtle differences between the twins.
如果你仔細地看，你還是可以看到這對雙胞胎有些小小的不同。

---

3. lean [lin] (v.) ｜ 傾斜；斜靠在

Gina leaned her head on Tommy's shoulder.
吉娜把頭靠在湯米的肩膀上。

---

4. shiver [ˈʃivə] (v.) ｜ 發抖，打顫

The boy stood shivering in the icy winter wind.
那男孩站在冰冷的冬天寒風中發抖。

---

5. command [kəˈmænd] (v.)/(n.) ｜ 命令，指揮

General MacArthur commanded the U.S. Army during World War II.
麥克阿瑟將軍在二次世界大戰期間負責指揮美國陸軍。

6. elect [ɪˈlɛkt] (v.) │ 選舉，推選

名詞是 election。

Kennedy was elected president, <u>edging out</u> Nixon by a mere 100,000 votes.
甘迺迪選上總統，僅以十萬票之差險勝尼克森。

....

7. happen overnight │ 一夜之間發生

Social media success doesn't happen overnight. It takes months, sometimes years, of hard work and dedication.
社群媒體上的成功並非一夜發生，得花上數個月、有時好幾年的努力和投入。

* dedication [ˌdɛdɪˈkeʃən] (n.) │ 奉獻，投入

....

8. strike up a conversation (with sb.) │ 開始（跟某人）交談

While waiting for the bus, Bob struck up a conversation with the lady sitting next to him.
鮑伯在等公車的時候，跟坐在他旁邊的女士聊了起來。

....

9. force [fɔrs] (v.) │ 強迫，迫使

The boss forced us to work weekends until the project was finished.
老闆強迫我們週末加班，直到專案結束為止。

....

10. push (one's/the) boundaries │ 挑戰極限

把界線（boundary）往外推（push），意思就是「挑戰某人的極限」。

(Jenny and Gina have been jogging in the park for five minutes.)
Gina: Wait, wait, I need to stop. This is killing me.
Jenny: Come on, Gina. You gotta keep pushing your boundaries if you wanna build up your stamina.

（珍妮和吉娜在公園裡跑步跑了五分鐘。）
吉娜：等等！我得停下來，我快累死了。
珍妮：不是吧，吉娜，妳如果想要增加體力，就要一直挑戰妳的極限。

* stamina [ˈstæmənə] (n.) │ 耐力，持久力

11. far from | 遠不及，差得遠

Gina is far from being fit—she can't even run for five minutes straight.
吉娜距離體力良好還差得遠，她連跑五分鐘都有問題。

....

12. charismatic [ˌkærɪzˈmætɪk] *(adj.)* | 有魅力的，有吸引力的

Jenny is a very charismatic person, both on and off the stage.
珍妮是相當有魅力的人，無論舞臺上下都是。

正能量
座右銘
MOTTO

Honor your father and your mother, so that you may live
long in the land the Lord your God is giving you.

當孝敬父母，使你的日子在耶和華你神所賜你的地上得以
長久。

—— 《聖經》出埃及記 20:12

A ¹Tribute to M

向爸媽致意

❶ dime

（美國或加拿大的）十分錢硬幣，一角硬幣。美國不同面額的銅板都有各自的名稱，一分錢硬幣叫 penny，五分錢硬幣是 nickel，十分錢硬幣是 dime，二十五分錢硬幣是 quarter，至於金錢單位「分」則稱作 cent，一百分錢等同於一美金（dollar）。

There are a couple of <u>specific</u> scenes I still remember from when I was a little kid. One is my dad waking me up in the middle of the night to say goodbye. Another one is my mom handing me cherries in a restaurant parking lot. These are both ²**vivid** memories of my childhood growing up in the United States.

My mom and dad met each other in college in Taiwan. They got married and had me several years later. That was before they sold everything they owned to continue their studies in the U.S.. My first memories of life in America go back to kindergarten. Our family of three lived in a dorm for overseas students called Lincoln Apartments. That's where my sister Joanna was born. It must have been tough ³**pursuing** degrees while raising two kids in a foreign country. I remember my mom always looking ⁴**stressed out**, especially when she had a paper due and me and my sis were screaming like crazy in the living room. And then my mom would start screaming like crazy at us. We'd stay quiet for a while, but kids are kids, so after a while the cycle would start all over again.

My parents' ⁵**finances** must have been tight too. Most of our furniture, from the sofa and bed frame to the dining table and desk, were all collected from the community ⁶**dumpster**. My mom ⁷**sewed** the curtains from cloth she bought at a yard sale. Every ❶**dime** had to be spent wisely.

Yet when I was little, I hardly ever felt like we were living on <u>a tight budget</u>. I went to school. I had my own bicycle, baseball glove, Ninja Turtles action <u>figures</u>. My parents even bought me my first Nintendo

⁸**console** when I was in second or third grade. And even though I only had a couple of ⁹**game cartridges**, my best friend Elliot had <u>thirty-something</u> of those. So if I really wanted to play new video games, I could just ¹⁰**drop by** Elliot's house. ¹¹**As far as I was concerned**, I had it all. Yes, I had a happy childhood.

When I look back on this period of my life, perhaps the only thing that gives me a clue about how hard my parents worked to support our family are the memories I mentioned in the first paragraph. My dad would get up at midnight every night, say goodbye to me, and go work the ^❷**graveyard shift** at a nursing home. At the time, he had three other part-time jobs. My mom waited tables at a Chinese restaurant to help <u>make ends meet</u>. On special <u>occasions</u>, when me and dad went to ¹²**pick her up** after work, she would give me a handful of sweet cherries. I didn't understand how hard it must have been back when I was a child. But now that I'm all grown up and understand how money and the world works, I'm truly amazed that my parents <u>made it</u> through those years. And I'm also ¹³**immensely** <u>grateful</u>. Thank you, mom and dad. I love you. Oops, ¹⁴**goose bumps**.

※ 底線單字為「複習單字」，為之前出現過的字。

❷ graveyard shift

大夜班。shift 是「值班時段」，graveyard 是「墓園」，兩者合在一起是「大夜班」的意思。英文裡的值班時段大致可以分成 the first, second, third shift，依序是「日班」、「下午班」、「晚班」，英文又可以稱為 day/regular shift, swing/evening shift, night shift。再細分的話，還有 morning shift「早班」，晚班又分為小夜班、大夜班，前者一般直接講 night shift，而「大夜班」就是 graveyard shift。至於「輪班」怎麼說呢？可以說 work (in) shifts 或 work rotating shifts，「週末班」是 weekend shift，「週間班」是 weekday shift，要「隨時待命」的則是 on-call shift。

JR的話

英文裡沒有對應「孝順」的單字，美國教育也不總是強調「孝順父母」。不過，在美國生活的孩子，會尊敬並喜愛自己的父母，也常把「愛」表達出來，這是跟東方教育很不一樣的地方。

A Tribute to
Mom and Dad
向爸媽致意

一直到現在，我都還清楚記得幾個小時候的特定畫面。一個是我爸半夜叫我起床、跟我說再見的畫面。另一個是我媽在一家餐廳停車場遞給我櫻桃的畫面。這兩件事是我在美國長大的童年裡，栩栩如生的記憶。

我爸媽是在臺灣的大學認識的，他們結婚幾年之後就生下了我。那是在他們將一切賣掉、到美國念書之前的事情。我在美國生活的第一份記憶是我幼稚園的時候。我們一家三口住在留學生宿舍林肯公寓的一個房子裡。那裡也是我妹妹Joanna出生的地方。在他鄉求學並同時照顧兩個孩子想必非常辛苦。我記得我媽看起來總是很焦慮，尤其當她有報告要交，偏偏我跟我妹又發瘋似地大肆尖叫到要把客廳掀翻的時候。接著，我媽就會對我們發瘋似地大罵一番。我們會安靜一下子，不過孩子就是孩子，不過一會兒又吵起來然後重複這個奇妙的循環。

我爸媽當時的經濟狀況想必也是相當拮据。家裡多數家具，從沙發到床架，餐桌到書桌，都是從社區垃圾場搬回來的。家中窗簾是我媽從跳蚤拍賣市場買布自己縫製的。每分錢都是花在刀口上。

不過，當時我並沒有感覺到家裡過得辛苦。我能上學。我有我自己的腳踏車、棒球手套、忍者龜玩具公仔。我爸媽甚至還在我二年級還三年級的時候買了第一個任天堂遊戲主機給我。即使我只有一兩個卡匣可以玩，而我朋友Elliot大概有三十幾個吧。所以如果我真的想玩新遊戲，我只要去Elliot家玩就好。我自己覺得，我擁有一切啊。是的，我有個快樂的童年。

當我回首這段日子，或許，唯一讓我察覺到我爸媽其實非常辛苦養家的線索，只有在第一段提到的那兩個回憶吧。我爸那時候每天晚上都會在凌晨12點起床跟我說再見，然後去老人安養中心做大夜班的工作。當時他還另外兼了三份差。我媽則是在中國餐館當服務生以維持生計。在某些特定節日，當我和爸爸去接她下班時，我媽會給我一堆甜美可口的櫻桃。我當時並不明白，那段時間有多苦。不過現在，我已經長大成人，了解金錢和這世界運作的方式。我對於我父母能度過那段日子感到相當讚嘆。我也滿懷感謝。謝謝你們，爸媽，我愛你們。噢，雞皮疙瘩都起來了。

Vocabulary & Phrases
單字片語

※ 底線單字為「複習單字」，為之前出現過的字。

1. tribute [ˋtrɪbjut] *(n.)* │ **稱頌，表達敬意的言辭、事物**

People left flowers as tributes to those lost in the earthquake.
人們獻花向那些在地震中喪生的人們致意。

2. vivid [ˋvɪvɪd] *(adj.)* │ **栩栩如生的，鮮活生動的**

I still have these vivid dreams of riding a unicorn above the clouds.
直到現在，我還會夢見我在雲上騎著獨角獸的栩栩如生畫面。

3. pursue [pɚˋsu] *(v.)* │ **追求；從事，實行**

Aside from her day job, Jenny is also pursuing a career as a dancer.
在平日工作之外，珍妮還從事舞者的工作。

4. stressed (out) [strɛst] *(adj.)* │ **緊張的，焦慮的，擔心的**

Jack:	God, I'm so stressed out! I just got chewed out by one of our clients.
Tommy:	Keep it together, man. You took one for the team.

傑克：天啊，我焦慮到爆了！我剛剛被客戶罵了一頓。

湯米：撐住啊，老兄，你犧牲小我完成大我了。

* **chew out** │（口語）責罵，斥責

* **take one for the team** │（口語）為了團隊利益而犧牲個人利益，意思近似於「犧牲小我」。

5. finances [ˈfaɪ.næns.ɪz] *(n.)* │（個人或公司）財源，財力，財務狀況

注意，這裡要用複數表示。單數 finance 是「金融」或「財務管理」的意思。

The finances of many households <u>took a beating</u> when the real estate market crashed in 2008.
2008 年房地產市場崩盤時，許多家庭的財務狀況受到很大打擊。

* real estate │房地產

----

6. dumpster [ˈdʌmpstɚ] *(n.)* │大型垃圾桶，廢料桶

I can't believe I found a brand new iPhone in the dumpster!
我不敢相信我在垃圾桶裡找到了一支全新的 iPhone 手機！

----

7. sew [so] *(v.)* │縫；做針線活

Her grandmother sewed her teddy bear's arm back on after she accidentally pulled it off.
她祖母將她不小心扯下來的泰迪熊手臂縫了回去。

----

8. console [ˈkɑnsol] *(n.)* │（電子設備或機器的）操控臺，儀表板，遊戲主機

The DJs were warned not to eat in the studio in case someone dropped food on the extremely expensive console.
DJ 們被警告不可以在播音室裡吃東西，以免有人把食物掉在那極度昂貴的控制臺上。

----

9. game cartridge │遊戲卡匣

cartridge 是「（設備中可替換的）芯，囊，管，筒」，所以 game cartridge 是「電動遊戲卡匣」，ink/printer cartridge 則是「墨水匣」。

----

10. drop by │順道拜訪

If you're ever in town, be sure to drop by and see me.
如果你哪天來市區，記得順道來我這裡坐坐。

11. as far as sb./sth. is concerned │ 在……看來，就……而言

As far as I'm concerned, if Bob has feelings for Jenny, he should let her know.
我個人認為，鮑伯對珍妮有意思的話，就應該對她表白。

* **have feelings for sb.** │ 對某人有感覺

......

12. pick sb. up │ 接某人

另一種意思則是「把某人，釣某人」。

Bob:　　 Last night I picked Jenny up...
Tommy:　Oh, you picked her up, did you?
Bob:　　 Hey! Don't twist my words! I <u>literally</u> picked her up and gave her a ride to her performance 'cause her car broke down.

鮑伯：昨晚我去接珍妮……
湯米：哦，你去搭訕珍妮，是嗎？
鮑伯：喂！不要曲解我的話！我真的是去接她，送她去參加表演，因為她的車子拋錨了。

* **twist one's words** │ 曲解某人的話

......

13. immensely [ɪˋmɛnslɪ] *(adv.)* │ 非常，極其

Jack felt immensely awkward on his first date with Jill.
傑克第一次跟茱兒約會時，感到超級尷尬。

......

14. goose bumps │ 雞皮疙瘩，或作 goosebumps

Tommy:　Babe, I love you more than the sun, moon and stars.
Gina:　　Cut it out, Casanova. You're giving me the goose bumps.

湯米：寶貝，我愛妳超過天上的太陽、月亮和星星。
吉娜：別鬧了，大情聖。你害我都起雞皮疙瘩了。

* **cut it out** │（口語）別鬧了、別說了
* **Casanova** [ˌkæzəˋnovə] │ 卡薩諾瓦是歐洲十八世紀公認的風流才子，後世將他的名字作為「大情聖」的意思。

More Expressions

JR's Choice JR 愛用的片語

a long list of ｜ 一長串的，很多的

事情多到可以寫成長長的清單，表示「很多」的意思。

Stella has a long list of complaints about her husband.

史黛拉對她老公的怨言可以列一大長串清單了。

at stake ｜ 有風險；處於危急關頭

Millions of lives will be at stake if the virus isn't stopped.

如果疫情不停止的話，將有數百萬生命受到危害。

by far ｜ 大大地

Ironman is by far the strongest superhero.

鋼鐵人絕對是最強的超級英雄
（遠勝過其他超級英雄）。

gear up ｜ 上緊發條，準備好迎接某事物

gear 是「裝備」的意思，gear up 就是「上緊發條，準備好迎接某事物」的意思。

Shopping malls are gearing up for the holiday season.

購物商場正準備迎接耶誕假期。

flesh out ｜ 充實（內容）

把一件只有大致骨架的事物用肉（flesh）填滿，就是 flesh out 的字面意義，也就是「用更多資訊和細節來充實」的意思。

After writing an outline for this book, it took me countless months to flesh out the content.

寫完本書摘要之後，
我花了無數個月的時間寫出裡面的內容。

far-fetched (adj.) ｜ 牽強的

Don't you think it's a bit far-fetched to say that Ironman is the strongest superhero?

你不覺得說鋼鐵人是最強超級英雄有點牽強嗎？

for real ｜（口語）真的；認真的

He's dating Natasha? For real?

他在跟娜塔莎約會？真的假的啊？

get on one's nerves ｜ 惹毛某人

不斷地觸動某人的神經（nerves），意味著「使某人感到煩躁」。

You're getting on my nerves. Leave me alone!

你搞得我很煩，離我遠一點！

get one's act together | 振作起來

My life is a mess. I really need to get my act together.

我的生活一團糟，我真的需要振作一下精神。

gloss over | 掩飾，掩蓋；避免談論某件令人不開心的事

He always glosses over his first relationship. I think he was hurt bad.

談到他第一段感情，他總是含糊其詞，我想他應該傷得很深。

get / wake up on the wrong side of the bed | 有起床氣；吃錯藥不開心

早上起床的時候下錯邊就容易有起床氣，衍伸為「無來由地心情不好、生氣」。

Don't mess with him. He got up on the wrong side of the bed today.

不要鬧他，他今天不知道哪一根筋不對。

give sth. a try / go | 嘗試做某事

There's a new ice cream flavor. We should give it a try.

有新的冰淇淋口味，我們應該要嚐看看。

got game | （尤指運動方面）技術很厲害

Man, he's got game! He beat me 6-0.

天啊，他好厲害！我被六比零打敗了。

get / have one's (own) way | 事事順己意

總是要別人遷就自己的意思。

You can't always have your way. You're gonna have to learn to work with others.

你不能總是要大家對你百依百順。
你得學會團隊合作。

in one's blood | 與生俱來的

表示「天生的，與生俱來的」；也可以說 in the / one's genes (基因)。

You have such a great singing voice. It must be in your blood!

你歌聲超好聽的，根本就是天生的！

it goes without saying 不言而喻，不用說也知道

It goes without saying that he's a natural singer.

不用說也知道，他是天生的歌手。

keep one's feet on the ground | 腳踏實地

Son, don't have your head in the clouds; always keep your feet on the ground like me.

孩子，絕對不要天馬行空、不切實際，
要像我一樣腳踏實地。

measure up | 符合，達到標準

I'll never measure up to my boss's expectations.

我永遠都無法達到我老闆的期待。

no way (, José) | (口語)決不，不可能

口語常在後面加一個西班牙文名字 José（念 Ho-Zay），聽起來比較活潑，帶有委婉拒絕的口吻。

....

Tony: Do you smoke?
Alex: No way, José.

東尼：你會抽菸嗎？
艾力克斯：決不，老兄。

---

out of one's mind | 瘋了；傻了

....

Are you out of your mind? You can't trust Tony.

你瘋了嗎？你不能相信東尼啦。

---

on paper | 理論上

....

The tactic looks good on paper, but we'll see how it goes on the field.

這戰術理論上看來很不錯，上了球場就知道是不是真的。

---

out of place | (某情況或場合)不適當，不妥當

....

I feel at little out of place at my new school.

我在新學校感到有點格格不入。

---

talk back (to sb.) | (對某人)頂嘴

....

Don't talk back to your teacher unless you wanna get in trouble.

不要跟老師頂嘴，除非你想自找麻煩。

---

piss sb. off | 讓某人氣炸

....

You're pissing me off!

你要把我氣瘋了！

---

steal the show | 出盡風頭

把整個秀（show）都偷走了（steal），意味著「出盡風頭」。

....

Your performance was perfect. You totally stole the show!

你的表演簡直是完美，完全出盡風頭！

---

take sth. for granted
把某事視為理所當然

....

Don't take your parents for granted. Cherish each moment you have with them.

不要把父母視為理所當然，
要珍惜每個擁有他們的時刻。

---

throw sb. under the bus | 害某人

什麼叫做把某人丟到巴士底下？類似中文的「拖某人下水」，但又不盡然，因為也有可能是本人沒有受到損害的情況下，把對方「推入火坑」，所以比較近似於「害某人」的意思。

....

I can't believe you threw me under the bus after all I've done for you!

在我為你付出了這麼多之後，
我不敢相信你這樣陷害我！

That's rich! | 真荒唐!真可笑!

太不切實際到讓人感到好笑。

....

Tony: Sam says he's the best-looking guy at school.
Alex: That's rich!

東尼:山姆說他是全校最帥的男生。
艾力克斯:是在搞笑喔?

suck it up | 坦然承受

坦然接受某個不開心的情況而不抱怨,有點類似中文的「打落牙齒和血吞」。

....

I know you failed the exam, but you gotta suck it up and move on.

我知道你考試落榜了,
但是你得打落牙齒和血吞,從失敗中走出來。

EZ TALK

JR Lee 正能量英文

作　　者：JR Lee
審　　訂：Judd Piggott
企劃責編：鄭莉璇
校　　對：鄭莉璇、JR Lee
裝幀設計：白日設計
內頁排版：張靜怡
行銷企劃：陳品萱

發 行 人：洪祺祥
副總經理：洪偉傑
副總編輯：曹仲堯
法律顧問：建大法律事務所
財務顧問：高威會計事務所

出　　版：日月文化出版股份有限公司
製　　作：EZ 叢書館
地　　址：臺北市信義路三段 151 號 8 樓
電　　話：(02) 2708-5509
傳　　真：(02) 2708-6157
網　　址：www.heliopolis.com.tw
郵撥帳號：19716071 日月文化出版股份有限公司

總 經 銷：聯合發行股份有限公司
電　　話：(02) 2917-8022
傳　　真：(02) 2915-7212
印　　刷：中原造像股份有限公司
初　　版：2020 年 7 月
初版10刷：2022 年 6 月
定　　價：380 元
Ｉ Ｓ Ｂ Ｎ：978-986-248-897-3

JR Lee 正能量英文／JR Lee 著 .
-- 初版 . -- 臺北市：日月文化 , 2020.07
240 面；16.7×23 公分（EZ Talk）
ISBN 978-986-248-897-3（平裝）
1. 成功法　2. 英語
177.2　　　　　　　　　109008113